Lee Canter's

ASSERTIVE DISCIPLINE®

Elementary Workbook

Grades K–6

Solution Tree | Press

a division of
Solution Tree

555 North Morton Street
Bloomington, IN 47404
800.733.6786 (toll free) / 812.336.7700
FAX: 812.336.7790

email: info@solution-tree.com
solution-tree.com

Cover design by Pam Rude

Printed in the United States of America

FSC

Mixed Sources

Product group from well-managed forests and other controlled sources

Cert no. SW-COC-002283
www.fsc.org
© 1996 Forest Stewardship Council

ISBN: 978-1-934009-16-1

Table of Contents

Preface

Assertive Discipline® is a highly regarded classroom behavior management program that was first developed in 1976. Over time, the program has evolved to meet the changing needs of today's classrooms. The focus of the Assertive Discipline program is on teaching students to assume responsibility for their own behavior. With this proactive and preventive approach, teachers can go beyond establishing basic discipline in their classrooms to creating cooperative environments in which students learn to choose appropriate, responsible behavior.

This *Assertive Discipline Elementary Workbook* is your guide to implementing the Assertive Discipline program, as described in the book *Assertive Discipline: Positive Behavior Management for Today's Classroom, Third Edition.* The easy-to-follow format presents brief overviews of the program's key points, as well as reproducible forms, positive notes, awards, badges, bookmarks, coupons, tracking sheets, communication and documentation pages, and visual aids that will allow you to successfully integrate the program into your teaching routine.

The job of an elementary teacher is challenging—especially in today's world. You may find, like many teachers today, that it is increasingly difficult to establish a classroom environment free of disruptive behavior.

But in spite of the difficulties you face, you can create and maintain the kind of classroom in which you can effectively teach and your students can learn and grow academically and socially.

How can you achieve this? By approaching the management of classroom behavior in a proactive manner. Whatever the age of your students, they will behave more responsibly and have more success at school if you give as much thought and planning to behavior management as you do to any instructional or curriculum practice. To become more proactive, you will want to follow these guidelines:

➤ Build positive, trusting relationships with your students by establishing yourself as a teacher who cares about their well-being in and out of school.

➤ Establish rules and specific directions that clearly define the limits of acceptable and unacceptable student behavior.

➤ Teach your students to consistently follow these rules and directions—to choose to behave responsibly—throughout the school day and the school year.

➤ Provide students with consistent recognition when they do behave. All children are eager for your positive words of encouragement and support.

➤ Adopt a positive, assertive manner when responding to students. Young students trust and respect the calm, consistent, and caring presence of an assertive teacher. They know that the teacher has a set of limits and that he or she will follow through appropriately whenever a student chooses not to behave. There is no confusion, no second-guessing, no hostility, and no anger.

➤ Remember to ask parents and administrators for their assistance when their support is needed. You can't do it alone. Education is a cooperative effort between teacher, student, parents, and administrators. Rely on each other for the positive assistance you can give.

Make the most of these formative years in elementary school. Create an atmosphere in which student self-esteem can flourish and you can feel accomplished at the end of each day. Become a positive, proactive teacher—today!

Creating Your Classroom Discipline Plan

This section of the *Assertive Discipline Elementary Workbook* looks at the classroom discipline plan—what it is and what it can do for you and your students. You will then develop a discipline plan for your own classroom with rules, supportive feedback, and corrective actions that best fit your needs and the needs of your students.

Also included in this section are a wide variety of reproducibles that will help you successfully develop and implement your classroom discipline plan.

What Is a Classroom Discipline Plan?

A classroom discipline plan is a system that allows you to spell out the behaviors you expect from students and what they can expect from you in return. The plan provides a framework around which all your classroom behavior management efforts can be organized.

The goal of a classroom discipline plan is to have a fair and consistent way to establish a safe, orderly, positive classroom environment in which you can teach and students can learn.

A classroom discipline plan consists of three parts:

1. **Rules** that students must follow at all times

2. **Supportive feedback** that students will receive for following the rules

3. **Corrective actions** that you will use when students choose not to follow the rules

---

Sample Classroom Discipline Plan
Elementary

Classroom Rules
Follow directions.
Keep hands, feet, and objects to yourself.
No teasing or name calling.

Supportive Feedback
Verbal recognition
Individual rewards, such as:
    First in line for recess
    Positive notes sent home to parents
    Positive phone calls to parents
    Positive notes to students
    Eat lunch with teacher
Classwide rewards

Corrective Actions

First time a student breaks a rule:	Reminder
Second time:	5 minutes working away from group, near teacher
Third time:	10 minutes working away from group
Fourth time:	Teacher calls parents
Fifth time:	Send to principal
Severe clause:	Send to principal

Benefits of a Classroom Discipline Plan

Here are four reasons why a classroom discipline plan will help you create a learning environment in your classroom that benefits both you and your students.

1. A discipline plan makes managing student behavior consistent.

Planning is the key to successful classroom management. When you have a plan for how you will respond to student behavior, you won't have to make on-the-spot decisions about what to do when a student misbehaves—or how to properly recognize a student who does behave appropriately. You will know what to do, your students will know what to expect, and the guesswork (and stress) will be eliminated from your daily disciplinary efforts.

A plan also provides the basis for teaching self-management. When the system for required school behavior is taught up front to the class, students then have the responsibility to use self-control and make good choices.

2. A discipline plan protects students' rights.

All students have rights to the same due process in the classroom. A discipline plan will help ensure that you respond to each student in a fair and consistent manner.

3. A discipline plan increases the likelihood of parental support.

When you communicate your discipline plan to parents, you let them know that you care about teaching their children to behave responsibly. This is a powerful message of support and professionalism to give to parents. Parents are more likely to give support (if you need it) when they know you are using an equitable system for all students.

4. A discipline plan helps ensure administrator support.

A discipline plan demonstrates to your administrator that you have a well-thought-out course of action for managing student behavior in your classroom. When your administrator understands the commitment you've made to effective classroom management, you will be better able to get support when you need it.

✎ It's Your Turn

The rest of this section will take you through the steps of creating a classroom discipline plan that is tailor-made for you and your students.

First, you will plan the general rules for your classroom.

Second, you will choose the supportive feedback you will use to motivate students to follow those rules.

Finally, you will learn how to most effectively correct students' behavior when they are not following the rules.

Create Rules

Whether kindergartners or fifth graders, your students all share something in common when they arrive in your classroom—each brings a variety of behavioral expectations from home and from previous teachers.

These expectations, however, may not be *your* behavioral expectations.

Your students can't be expected to know how you want them to behave in your classroom unless you make these expectations clear to them. General classroom rules, therefore, are the first part of your classroom discipline plan.

What Are General Classroom Rules?

General classroom rules are those rules that are in place all day long—throughout all activities. They are important because they let your students know what basic behavioral expectations you have. Successful teachers have a minimal number of rules that are in effect at all times, in all activities, all day long. The following guidelines will help you choose appropriate classroom rules.

Choose rules that are observable and continually in effect.

Address behaviors that you can clearly see. Vaguely stated expectations may mean one thing to one child and an entirely different thing to another. As a result, they often cause problems by opening the door to arguments.

Observable Rules

➤ Keep hands and feet to yourself.

➤ Be in line when the bell rings.

➤ No yelling or screaming.

Vague Expectations

➤ Be kind to other students.

➤ No fooling around when class starts.

➤ No unnecessary talking.

Choose rules that apply throughout the entire day.

General classroom rules are rules that apply all day, no matter what activity is taking place. These are rules that students are expected to follow at all times.

Now, before you choose your own rules, take a look on page 5 at some rules that are *not* appropriate general classroom rules. Though often seen in classrooms, these rules are not appropriate general classroom rules because they are not applicable throughout the entire day. Notice that while each rule *sounds* sensible, it cannot be a realistic ongoing expectation.

Avoid these rules.

Raise your hand and wait to be called on before you speak. There are going to be times when students are expected to speak out (for example, when working in groups). Therefore, it is not an appropriate general classroom rule.

Stay in your seat unless you have permission to get up. There may be many times during the day when it is okay for a student to get up without asking permission (for example, when she is sharpening a pencil, or when he has completed a book and is returning it to the shelf). Again, this rule would not be enforceable throughout the day.

Use a 12-inch voice in the classroom. Of course there will be times when students need to speak up! Do not make voice-level requirements part of your general classroom rules.

Complete all homework assignments. This rule does not relate to classroom behavior, and there may be times when completing homework is out of a student's control.

When you establish general classroom rules that do not clearly reflect your consistent expectations, you run the risk of confusing students, and you will not be able to enforce these rules with consistency.

Establish general classroom rules appropriate for elementary students.

Notice that each of these rules is applicable throughout the entire day and that each one is observable.

Grades K–3

➤ Follow directions.

➤ Keep hands, feet, and objects to yourself.

➤ Do not leave the room without permission.

➤ Use appropriate school language; no teasing or put-downs.

Grades 4–6

➤ Follow directions.

➤ Keep hands, feet, and objects to yourself.

➤ No swearing or teasing.

➤ No yelling.

 It's Your Turn

Use the "Classroom Rules Worksheet" on page 6 to plan the general classroom rules you will use in your own classroom. When you're finished, enlarge the "Our Classroom Rules" poster on page 7, and write your rules on it.

Classroom Rules Worksheet

Use this worksheet to plan your own general classroom rules. The list has been started for you with the rule "Follow directions." This is important because students must be expected to follow any directions you might give during the day. When choosing the rest of your rules, remember: 1) Rules must be observable, and 2) rules must apply throughout the entire day.

Classroom Rule: *Follow directions.*

This is an appropriate rule because:

_____

_____

_____

_____

Classroom Rule: _____

This is appropriate because:

_____

_____

_____

_____

Classroom Rule: _____

This is appropriate because:

_____

_____

_____

_____

Classroom Rule: _____

This is appropriate because:

_____

_____

_____

_____

Assertive Discipline Elementary Workbook
© 2002 Solution Tree Press • solution-tree.com

Use Supportive Feedback

Your general classroom rules are the first part of your classroom discipline plan. The second part of your classroom discipline plan, supportive feedback, will help you motivate your students to follow these rules.

Supportive feedback is the sincere and meaningful attention you give a student for behaving according to your expectations.

Supportive feedback is a powerful motivator for elementary-age students. Consistently used, supportive feedback will:

➤ Encourage your students to continue appropriate behavior.

➤ Dramatically reduce problem behaviors.

➤ Create a positive classroom environment for you and your students.

➤ Help you teach behavior and establish positive relationships with your students.

➤ Increase your students' self-esteem.

 Refer to *Assertive Discipline, Third Edition,* for an in-depth look at these benefits.

With these benefits in mind, let's take a look now at five ways you can provide supportive feedback to individual students:

1. Verbal recognition

2. Positive notes and phone calls home

3. Behavior awards

4. Special privileges

5. Tangible rewards

Verbal Recognition

You know that elementary-age students enjoy receiving verbal recognition from their teacher. An award, sticker, or special treat is always welcomed and appreciated. But the easiest, most meaningful means of supportive feedback you can give is verbal recognition.

When you take the time to say something positive in recognition of a student's achievement, you are making a statement that will have a long-lasting impact. You are saying, "I care about you. I notice the good work you are doing. I'm proud of you, and you should feel proud of yourself, too."

Verbal recognition should be your number-one choice when it comes to supporting your students' efforts in the classroom.

To make the recognition as effective as possible, keep the following guidelines in mind.

Verbal recognition should be personal.

Always include the student's name in your comments, and watch the smiles appear:

"Maria, you worked cooperatively with Lauren in your group today. Your entire assignment was completed."

Verbal recognition must be genuine.

Children know sincere words when they hear them. Make sure what you say genuinely reflects your feelings of pride in a student's accomplishments.

Verbal recognition is descriptive and specific.

Verbal recognition will be most effective when it refers to something specific the student has accomplished. "Samuel, thanks for your help in tutoring the first graders today" sounds more meaningful than "Great job, Samuel."

It's Your Turn

Start thinking now about all of the opportunities you have each day to verbally recognize your students' successes—all of the moments when an admiring word from you can make a big difference in a student's life. Jot notes in your plan book reminding yourself to look for students' good behavior, then say something about it!

Give timely reminders.

As an extra reminder to consistently recognize students, make a copy of the "The Time Is Right for Super Classroom Behavior!" poster on page 10. Hang this reminder on the classroom wall right next to the clock. The timely note will give you a nudge throughout the day to keep looking for positive behavior to reinforce.

Look for just the right moment to say "Good for you!"

There are hundreds of opportunities to recognize students each day of the year. Don't let these moments slip by. To help you further develop the habit, look over the list of "50 Opportunities to Say 'You're Terrific'" (see page 11). Keep this sheet in your desk or plan book, and review it from time to time as a reminder of all the occasions throughout the school day when you can verbally recognize a student's good behavior.

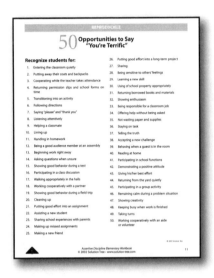

The time is right for super classroom behavior!

Assertive Discipline Elementary Workbook
© 2002 Solution Tree Press • solution-tree.com

 50 Opportunities to Say "You're Terrific"

Recognize students for:

1. Entering the classroom quietly
2. Putting away their coats and backpacks
3. Cooperating while the teacher takes attendance
4. Returning permission slips and school forms on time
5. Transitioning into an activity
6. Following directions
7. Saying "please" and "thank you"
8. Listening attentively
9. Helping a classmate
10. Lining up
11. Handing in homework
12. Being a good audience member at an assembly
13. Beginning work right away
14. Asking questions when unsure
15. Showing good behavior during a test
16. Participating in a class discussion
17. Walking appropriately in the halls
18. Working cooperatively with a partner
19. Showing good behavior during a field trip
20. Cleaning up
21. Putting good effort into an assignment
22. Assisting a new student
23. Sharing school experiences with parents
24. Making up missed assignments
25. Making a new friend
26. Putting good effort into a long-term project
27. Sharing
28. Being sensitive to others' feelings
29. Learning a new skill
30. Using school property appropriately
31. Returning borrowed books and materials
32. Showing enthusiasm
33. Being responsible for a classroom job
34. Offering help without being asked
35. Not wasting paper and supplies
36. Staying on task
37. Telling the truth
38. Accepting a new challenge
39. Behaving when a guest is in the room
40. Reading at home
41. Participating in school functions
42. Demonstrating a positive attitude
43. Giving his/her best effort
44. Returning from the yard quietly
45. Participating in a group activity
46. Remaining calm during a problem situation
47. Showing creativity
48. Keeping busy when work is finished
49. Taking turns
50. Working cooperatively with an aide or volunteer

Positive Notes and Phone Calls Home

Good news is always welcomed! It makes sense, then, that positive notes, emails, and phone calls be an important part of your supportive feedback plan.

The goal of a positive note or phone call is to share with parents "good news" about their child. Telling your students that you will send positive messages to parents about their good behavior is a great motivator. Few things are as important to children as knowing their parents are proud of them and the work they are doing.

It's also a great way to establish a positive relationship with parents. Throughout the year, you will need parental support. It will be much easier to gain that support when you need it if you have already begun building a positive foundation.

Positive phone calls and notes don't take much time, but they pay big dividends.

Here's what a positive phone call to a parent might sound like:

> "Mrs. Garson? This is Miss Wu, Jonathan's teacher. I want you to know that Jonathan is making a great start this school year. This first week, we've spent a lot of time learning to follow the classroom rules, and I am happy to let you know that Jonathan is following those rules and setting a great example for the other students.
>
> Please tell Jonathan I called and how pleased I am with his behavior in class."

It's just that easy and just that quick. In a few brief moments, this teacher has established a positive relationship with a parent and boosted the self-esteem of a student.

Dear Mr. and Mrs. Washington,

I am so pleased to let you know what a wonderful job Elise is doing in my class. She listens when directions are given, and follows directions quickly and quietly. That's very important when you're in a room with 30 children! This kind of responsible behavior will help Elise do a good job in her schoolwork. You should be very proud of the effort she's making.

Sincerely,

Miss Wu

It's Your Turn

Once you recognize how easy it really is to make positive contact with parents, you'll be convinced that it's an effective use of your time. The suggestions that follow will help you develop this positive parent involvement habit.

First, set goals!

Set a goal to make a specific number of positive phone calls and to send a specific number of notes home each week. (Just two contacts a day will ensure that you reach every parent with good news each month!) To make sure all students receive this important attention, keep track of your positive contacts by using the "Positive Parent Communication Log" on page 14.

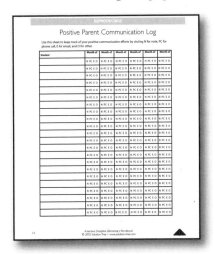

Next, remember the good things that happen!

Use the Positive Memos on page 15 to jot down positive comments you want to remember and later share with parents in a note or phone call. Run off copies of the memos and keep a stack close by your desk. During the day when something "memo"rable happens that you'd like to communicate, write it down! You may wish to keep this memo as part of a student's documentation file.

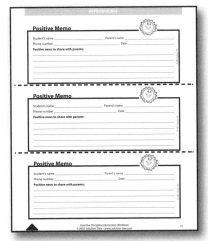

Finally, be sure to share the good news!

Use the reproducible positive notes on pages 17–22 any time you want parents and students to know how proud you are of student achievement. Run off copies of these reproducible notes, keep them handy, and use them frequently. (Keep track of the notes you sent home by using the Positive Parent Communication Log on page 14.)

Positive Parent Communication Log

Use this sheet to keep track of your positive communication efforts by circling N for note, PC for phone call, E for email, and O for other.

Student	Month of	Month of	Month of	Month of	Month of	Month of
	N PC E O	N PC E O	N PC E O	N PC E O	N PC E O	N PC E O
	N PC E O	N PC E O	N PC E O	N PC E O	N PC E O	N PC E O
	N PC E O	N PC E O	N PC E O	N PC E O	N PC E O	N PC E O
	N PC E O	N PC E O	N PC E O	N PC E O	N PC E O	N PC E O
	N PC E O	N PC E O	N PC E O	N PC E O	N PC E O	N PC E O
	N PC E O	N PC E O	N PC E O	N PC E O	N PC E O	N PC E O
	N PC E O	N PC E O	N PC E O	N PC E O	N PC E O	N PC E O
	N PC E O	N PC E O	N PC E O	N PC E O	N PC E O	N PC E O
	N PC E O	N PC E O	N PC E O	N PC E O	N PC E O	N PC E O
	N PC E O	N PC E O	N PC E O	N PC E O	N PC E O	N PC E O
	N PC E O	N PC E O	N PC E O	N PC E O	N PC E O	N PC E O
	N PC E O	N PC E O	N PC E O	N PC E O	N PC E O	N PC E O
	N PC E O	N PC E O	N PC E O	N PC E O	N PC E O	N PC E O
	N PC E O	N PC E O	N PC E O	N PC E O	N PC E O	N PC E O
	N PC E O	N PC E O	N PC E O	N PC E O	N PC E O	N PC E O
	N PC E O	N PC E O	N PC E O	N PC E O	N PC E O	N PC E O
	N PC E O	N PC E O	N PC E O	N PC E O	N PC E O	N PC E O
	N PC E O	N PC E O	N PC E O	N PC E O	N PC E O	N PC E O
	N PC E O	N PC E O	N PC E O	N PC E O	N PC E O	N PC E O
	N PC E O	N PC E O	N PC E O	N PC E O	N PC E O	N PC E O
	N PC E O	N PC E O	N PC E O	N PC E O	N PC E O	N PC E O

Assertive Discipline Elementary Workbook
© 2002 Solution Tree Press • solution-tree.com

Positive Memo

Student's name _____ Parent's name _____

Phone number _____ Date _____

Positive news to share with parents:

_____

_____

_____

_____

_____

© 2002 Solution Tree

Positive Memo

Student's name _____ Parent's name _____

Phone number _____ Date _____

Positive news to share with parents:

_____

_____

_____

_____

© 2002 Solution Tree

Positive Memo

Student's name _____ Parent's name _____

Phone number _____ Date _____

Positive news to share with parents:

_____

_____

_____

_____

© 2002 Solution Tree

Behavior Awards

Special awards for good behavior are always a great motivator for elementary-age students because they have a double impact!

1. Students will be proud to receive them from you.

2. They'll also be proud to take them home to show parents!

Tell students that one way you'll recognize good behavior throughout the year is by sending home special awards that let them and their parents know how responsibly they are behaving in school.

To keep yourself on track, plan to send home a specific number of awards each week.

 It's Your Turn

Starting on page 23, you will find a variety of behavior awards designed especially for elementary students.

➤ **Primary students** will enjoy receiving the "good behavior" badges on page 23 and bookmarks on page 24.

➤ **Upper elementary students** will appreciate the bookmarks on pages 25–26.

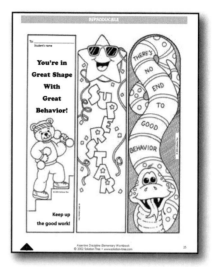

➤ **All students**, and their parents, will appreciate the behavior certificates on pages 27–33—certificates that are sure to be proudly displayed at home and later kept in scrapbooks. Just fill in the good behavior you want to recognize, and present the award to the deserving student!

QUICK NOTE
to Parents

To: _____

Just a quick note to tell you
how pleased I am that _____

_____

_____

_____

_____

_____

Signed   Date

© 2002 Solution Tree

QUICK NOTE
to Parents

To: _____

Just a quick note to tell you
how pleased I am that _____

_____

_____

_____

_____

_____

Signed   Date

© 2002 Solution Tree

QUICK NOTE
to Parents

To: _____

Just a quick note to tell you
how pleased I am that _____

_____

_____

_____

_____

_____

Signed   Date

© 2002 Solution Tree

QUICK NOTE
to Parents

To: _____

Just a quick note to tell you
how pleased I am that _____

_____

_____

_____

_____

_____

Signed   Date

© 2002 Solution Tree

QUICK NOTE
to Students

To: _____

Just a quick note to let you know

_____

_____

_____

_____

_____

_____

Signed _____ Date _____

QUICK NOTE
to Students

To: _____

Just a quick note to let you know

_____

_____

_____

_____

_____

_____

Signed _____ Date _____

QUICK NOTE
to Students

To: _____

Just a quick note to let you know

_____

_____

_____

_____

_____

_____

Signed _____ Date _____

QUICK NOTE
to Students

To: _____

Just a quick note to let you know

_____

_____

_____

_____

_____

_____

Signed _____ Date _____

Assertive Discipline Elementary Workbook
© 2002 Solution Tree Press • solution-tree.com

FLYING HIGH WITH GOOD BEHAVIOR!!!

HEARTFELT THANKS FOR GOOD BEHAVIOR

GOOD BEHAVIOR MAKES YOU A STAR!

_____'s
Student's name

behavior is "purr-fectly" wonderful.

Thanks!

_____
Signed   Date

© 2002 Solution Tree

A little mouse told me that

_____
Student's name

always follows directions.

Thanks!

_____
Signed   Date

© 2002 Solution Tree

To: _____
Student's name

You're in Great Shape With Great Behavior!

© 2002 Solution Tree

Keep up the good work!

SUPER STAR

© 2002 Solution Tree

THERE'S NO END TO GOOD BEHAVIOR

© 2002 Solution Tree

It's no puzzle . . .
your behavior
is really together!

© 2002 Solution Tree

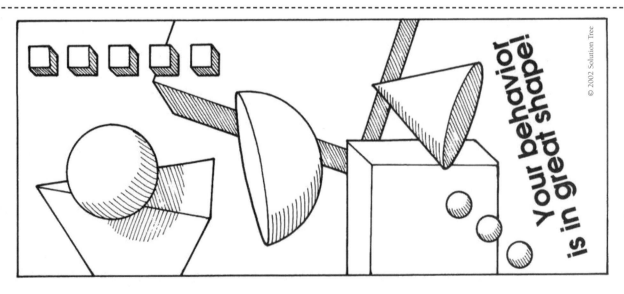

. . . your behavior
Great behavior!
it shines!

© 2002 Solution Tree

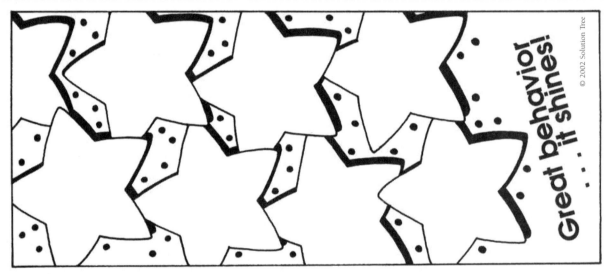

Your behavior
is in great shape!

© 2002 Solution Tree

Assertive Discipline Elementary Workbook
© 2002 Solution Tree Press • solution-tree.com

_____
Student's name

gets "high marks" for improved behavior because

_____

_____

_____

_____

Great job!

_____
Signed   Date

© 2002 Solution Tree

Your "royal" behavior is noticed because

_____

_____

_____

_____
Signed   Date

© 2002 Solution Tree

Assertive Discipline Elementary Workbook
© 2002 Solution Tree Press • solution-tree.com

THANKS

_____
Student's name

for _____

_____

_____

_____
Signed   Date

© 2002 Solution Tree

To:_____
Student's name

Your behavior is something to celebrate.

Thanks!

_____
Signed   Date

© 2002 Solution Tree

To: _____
Student's name

Thanks for _____

_____

_____

Signed _____ Date _____

© 2002 Solution Tree

School's a smooth ride when you behave like _____ .
Student's name

Signed _____ Date _____

© 2002 Solution Tree

Assertive Discipline Elementary Workbook
© 2002 Solution Tree Press • solution-tree.com

To:_____
        Student's name

I'd like to say a few words about the way you behave in class . . .

GOOD JOB!

TERRIFIC!

SUPER!

_____   _____
Signed   Date

© 2002 Solution Tree

To:_____
        Student's name

Your responsible behavior has made you a star!

Thanks!

_____   _____
Signed   Date

© 2002 Solution Tree

Special Privileges

Every student has something special that he or she enjoys doing at school. Some students love to be class monitor. Others appreciate free reading time. Still others find extra computer time a wonderful treat.

When you want to recognize positive student behavior and motivate your students to continue that behavior, allow them to take part in activities that they particularly enjoy.

What do your students like to do? Here are some ideas to get you started. Add ideas of your own on the lines that follow.

➤ Be first in line.

➤ Take care of the class pet.

➤ Be classroom monitor.

➤ Correct papers.

➤ Tutor young children.

➤ Help the teacher.

➤ Have free time.

➤ Receive extra computer time.

➤ Work on a favorite activity.

➤ _____

➤ _____

➤ _____

➤ _____

➤ _____

➤ _____

➤ _____

➤ _____

➤ _____

➤ _____

➤ _____

➤ _____

➤ _____

➤ _____

➤ _____

It's Your Turn

Just ask 'em!

Not sure what special privileges will motivate your students? Give students the "My Favorite Activities" menu on page 36. The menu includes some activities that take place in most classrooms. Add your own to the list, and ask students to check off three of their favorites. Older students can also write in suggestions of their own.

Tell students that you want them to make these "menu" selections because, throughout the year, you will be awarding special privileges to students who behave responsibly at school. Tie this activity to a brief class discussion and you're sure to gather lots of motivating suggestions!

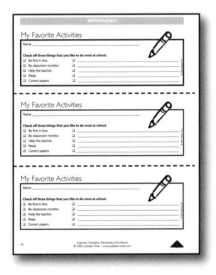

You earned it!

When a student earns a special privilege for good behavior, fill out a "You Earned It!" coupon (see page 37).

These open-ended coupons give students the good news and give you an easy way to present positive recognition.

Sprinkle in some praise with your presentation and make the recognition even more meaningful:

> "You followed my directions so well, Andy, that you've earned the privilege of being first in line for lunch. Here's your reward coupon."

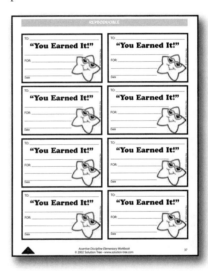

My Favorite Activities

Name _____

Check off three things that you like to do most at school.

❑ Be first in line.   ❑ _____
❑ Be classroom monitor.   ❑ _____
❑ Help the teacher.   ❑ _____
❑ Read.   ❑ _____
❑ Correct papers.   ❑ _____

© 2002 Solution Tree

- -

My Favorite Activities

Name _____

Check off three things that you like to do most at school.

❑ Be first in line.   ❑ _____
❑ Be classroom monitor.   ❑ _____
❑ Help the teacher.   ❑ _____
❑ Read.   ❑ _____
❑ Correct papers.   ❑ _____

© 2002 Solution Tree

- -

My Favorite Activities

Name _____

Check off three things that you like to do most at school.

❑ Be first in line.   ❑ _____
❑ Be classroom monitor.   ❑ _____
❑ Help the teacher.   ❑ _____
❑ Read.   ❑ _____
❑ Correct papers.   ❑ _____

© 2002 Solution Tree

Assertive Discipline Elementary Workbook
© 2002 Solution Tree Press • solution-tree.com

TO: _____

"You Earned It!"

_____

FOR: _____

_____

Date _____

© 2002 Solution Tree

TO: _____

"You Earned It!"

_____

FOR: _____

_____

Date _____

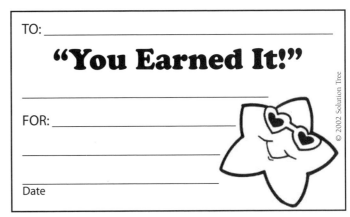

© 2002 Solution Tree

TO: _____

"You Earned It!"

_____

FOR: _____

_____

Date _____

© 2002 Solution Tree

TO: _____

"You Earned It!"

_____

FOR: _____

_____

Date _____

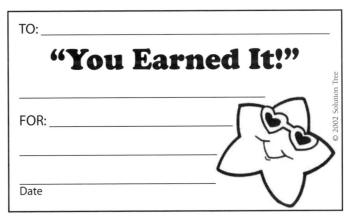

© 2002 Solution Tree

TO: _____

"You Earned It!"

_____

FOR: _____

_____

Date _____

© 2002 Solution Tree

TO: _____

"You Earned It!"

_____

FOR: _____

_____

Date _____

© 2002 Solution Tree

TO: _____

"You Earned It!"

_____

FOR: _____

_____

Date _____

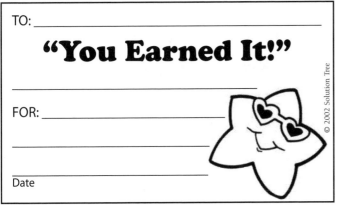

© 2002 Solution Tree

TO: _____

"You Earned It!"

_____

FOR: _____

_____

Date _____

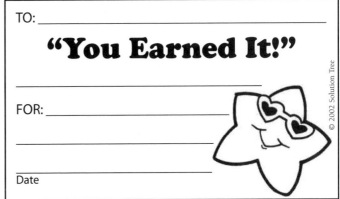

© 2002 Solution Tree

Tangible Rewards

Most students are motivated by verbal recognition, positive notes, and special privileges. You may, however, have one or two students who simply do not respond to these positive reinforcers. There are times when tangible rewards such as stickers or small trinkets are the only positives that will work—the only motivation a student will respond to. When needed, use tangible rewards, but use them with care.

Follow these guidelines:

➤ Be sure to give a tangible reward immediately after you have observed the desired behavior. You want the student to associate this behavior with the reward.

➤ Whenever you give a student a tangible reward, always pair it with your own verbal recognition, such as:

> "Bobby, here's a sticker for sitting so quietly. I'm really proud of you."

> "Kelly, here's a pencil topper for taking your seat so quickly and quietly when you came in the classroom. Because you came in so calmly, we were able to listen to the story right away."

➤ Use tangible rewards sparingly, or they will lose their effectiveness.

Tangible rewards are particularly effective on days when students tend to be overly excited, such as on Fridays and before holidays.

✎ It's Your Turn

We've looked at five ways you can positively support students for following the rules of the classroom:

1. Verbal recognition

2. Positive notes and phone calls home

3. Behavior awards

4. Special privileges

5. Tangible rewards

Now it's time to choose the supportive feedback you will use with individual students in your own classroom. Be sure to include positives that you are comfortable giving and, most importantly, ones that you will be able to give frequently and consistently.

When you're finished planning, enlarge the "Supportive Feedback" poster on page 39 and list the activities you will use to support students' appropriate behavior. (Tuck the finished poster away with your supplies. You'll be using it when you introduce your classroom discipline plan to your students.)

REPRODUCIBLE

SUPPORTIVE FEEDBACK

Assertive Discipline Elementary Workbook
© 2002 Solution Tree • www.solution-tree.com
39

SUPPORTIVE FEEDBACK

_____

_____

_____

_____

_____

_____

_____

_____

_____

Classwide Positive Recognition

Just as you recognize individual students for their appropriate behavior, you can also recognize your entire class for meeting expectations. A classwide positive recognition system makes it easy.

What is a classwide positive recognition system?

A classwide positive recognition system is a program in which all of your students, not just one student, work together toward a positive reward that will be given to the entire class.

The goal of a classwide recognition system is to motivate students to learn new behavior or work on improving a problem behavior.
It shows students how important it is to achieve a common goal. A classwide recognition system is especially effective at the beginning of the school year, when your goal is to create a cooperative, interdependent classroom community. You can also use a classwide recognition system during difficult months, such as December and June, when student behavior may be sliding.

Here's how to set up a classwide recognition system.

1. Pick a system that you are comfortable with and that is appropriate to the age of your students. (On pages 42–45, you will find directions and artwork for creating your own positive behavior bulletin board.)

2. Have students give input on the rewards; however, be sure to choose those you are comfortable giving. Whatever rewards you choose, make sure they are things the students will want to work toward.

   Here are some ideas for classwide rewards:

   ➢ Extra free time in class

   ➢ Special arts and crafts project

   ➢ Extra P.E. time

   ➢ Special movie or video with popcorn

   ➢ A special visitor

3. Start with simple privileges for the first month (such as free time in class or extra P.E. time). Save videos and treats for later in the school year.

4. Set a numerical goal for the class. Make sure students are able to attain the reward in a timely manner. Here are some suggested time frames for elementary students:

Grades K–1	1 day
Grades 2–3	2 days to 1 week
Grades 4–6	1 week

5. Be sure your program complies with school and district policies.

6. Once the class has earned points toward a classwide reward, do not take away points for misbehavior. In addition, all students, regardless of corrective actions that may have been necessary, should participate in the classwide reward. If you correct a student's behavior and then also take away the classwide reward, you are providing two consequences for one misbehavior.

Building Positive Relationships

Your supportive feedback—for both individual students and the entire class—will be greatly enhanced by the strength of your positive relationships with students. The adage "Students don't care how much you know until they know how much you care" particularly applies to your behavior management efforts. Building relationships with students doesn't just happen. You need to plan ways to reach out and get to know all of your students, even the most challenging ones.

Try some of these ideas:

➤ Greet your students by name each morning as they enter your classroom.

➤ Look for opportunities throughout the day to chat with students about issues of importance to them besides classwork.

➤ Take a student interest inventory at the beginning of the year to learn about your students' favorite activities (see page 46).

➤ Share appropriate personal information about yourself such as interests and experiences.

➤ Call a student after a bad day and discuss how the next day could be better.

➤ Call a student after a good day and compliment his or her success.

➤ Send get-well notes, or call home, if a student is sick.

➤ Write positive notes to students and their parents.

It's Your Turn

The following pages contain artwork and instructions for creating a positive behavior bulletin board, plus a student interest inventory that you can reproduce and distribute to your students.

We **"GOPHER"** Good Behavior
Bulletin Board

Suggestions for Construction

1. Draw the underground gopher tunnel on brown paper. Divide the tunnel into spaces equal to the number of days students must demonstrate good behavior in order to achieve their goal and receive their classwide reward.

   For example: Grades K–3, 5 spaces   Grades 4–5, 10 spaces

2. Draw a 12"-wide Finish Line hole where the tunnel emerges through the ground.

3. Make grass from strips of green construction paper. Staple or pin to board as shown.

4. Color and cut out the "We Gopher Good Behavior" sign (see page 43). Place sign at the beginning of the tunnel (see illustration).

5. Color and cut out the large gopher (see page 44).

6. (Optional) Reproduce the "I Dig Good Behavior" gopher tags—one per student (see page 45). Ask each student to color, cut out, and write his or her name on the gopher tag. Pin all gopher tags around the border of the bulletin board.

Suggestions for Use

The object of this classwide recognition system is for the class to "tunnel" through the underground maze by behaving appropriately in class. Encourage all students to participate in reaching the final goal by jotting down points on the chalkboard during the day. Whenever you notice the entire class or an individual student behaving appropriately, verbally recognize the student(s) and chalk up a point! At the end of the day, total the points. If the sum equals a predetermined number (such as 10, 20, or 30), move the large gopher one space ahead in the tunnel. The object of this activity is for the class to succeed every day and for the gopher to move through the tunnel in a week or two. Always be on the lookout for good behavior, especially with those difficult students who need positive recognition for their efforts. On the day the gopher emerges from the tunnel, reward the class with a special activity.

Room _____

We gather together

to study and learn

happy behavior.

We "gopher" good behavior

© 2002 Solution Tree

I "dig" good behavior!

© 2002 Solution Tree

I "dig" good behavior!

© 2002 Solution Tree

I "dig" good behavior!

© 2002 Solution Tree

I "dig" good behavior!

© 2002 Solution Tree

Student Interest Inventory

Name: _____

Today's Date: _____ Birth Date: _____

Brothers and Sisters:

Name _____ Age _____

Name _____ Age _____

Name _____ Age _____

Name _____ Age _____

Name _____ Age _____

Special friends: _____

_____

What I like to do most at home: _____

_____

These are my favorite hobbies: _____

_____

These are my favorites:

Book _____ TV show _____

Movie _____ Food _____

Singer _____ Song _____

If I had one wish, it would be: _____

School would be better if: _____

If I had a million dollars, I would: _____

_____

This is what my teacher did last year that I liked the most: _____

_____

This is what my teacher did last year that I liked the least: _____

_____

Assertive Discipline Elementary Workbook
© 2002 Solution Tree Press • solution-tree.com

Take Corrective Actions

In spite of the care you take in choosing your rules, and in spite of your consistent use of supportive feedback, there will be times when students will choose not to follow the rules of your classroom. When this disruptive behavior occurs, you must be prepared to respond calmly and quickly.

Corrective actions are the third part of your classroom discipline plan.

Why Are Corrective Actions Important?

By carefully planning in advance what you will do when students misbehave, you won't be caught off guard or left wondering how to respond to a student's misbehavior. And that means that students will be treated fairly and you will feel less stress.

Use the following guidelines when choosing corrective actions.

Corrective actions are fundamental for self-management.

Corrective actions are helpful tools in teaching students how to behave in your classroom. It's important that students understand that if they *choose* to misbehave, certain actions will occur. When you give students a choice, you place responsibility where it belongs—with the student.

For example:

Teacher:	Sara, our classroom rule is "No teasing." If you tease any student in this class, you will choose to sit by yourself and do your work. It's your choice.
Sara:	Okay. (*Within a minute, Sara is teasing Ryan, the student who sits next to her.*)
Teacher:	Sara, you're teasing Ryan. You have chosen to sit by yourself at the table in the back of the room.

Remember: *Choice* is the key word. When you give students a choice, they learn that they can be in control of what happens to them. Keep in mind that corrective actions are not punishment. They are actions students know will occur should they choose to break the rules of the classroom. Corrective actions must be seen as natural outcomes of inappropriate behavior.

Corrective actions do not have to be severe to be effective.

Teachers often think that the more severe the corrective action, the more impact it will have on a student. This is not true. The key to effective corrective actions is that they are used consistently. It is the inevitability of the corrective action that makes it effective. Minimal actions, such as 5 minutes working away from the group, can be as effective as after-school detention when they are given consistently.

> *Note:* Corrective actions must be things that students do not like, but they must never be physically or psychologically harmful.

Establishing a Discipline Hierarchy

The best way to use corrective actions is to organize them into a discipline hierarchy as part of your classroom discipline plan. When placed in a hierarchy, corrective actions guide students toward self-management.

> ➤ The hierarchy is progressive, starting with a verbal reminder.

> ➤ The corrective actions then become gradually more substantial for the second, third, fourth, and fifth time that a student chooses to disrupt within a day.

The discipline hierarchy works as follows.

First time a student disrupts

Give a reminder the first time a student disrupts or breaks a classroom rule.

A reminder is important because it gives the student an opportunity to choose more appropriate behavior before a more substantial corrective action occurs.

Second or third time a student disrupts

The second or third time a student disrupts in the same day, you need to provide a corrective action.

These actions should be easy to implement and not time-consuming. Typical corrective actions for second and third infractions include changing seats and sitting close to the teacher.

Fourth time a student disrupts

Four disruptions during one day are not acceptable. You need to contact parents if a student disrupts a fourth time in a day.

For some students, involving parents will be the only way you will motivate them to behave appropriately. Students need to

know that you will be consistent in the enforcement of this corrective action.

Fifth time a student disrupts

Sending a student to the principal should be the last corrective action on your discipline hierarchy.

In preparation for implementing this corrective action, you must have already met with the principal and discussed actions he or she will take when students are sent to the office.

Severe clause

Sometimes you have to act quickly and decisively to stop a student's disruptive behavior. In the case of severe misbehavior, such as fighting, vandalism, defying a teacher, or in some way stopping the entire class from functioning, a student will not receive a warning. He or she loses the right to proceed through the hierarchy. Severe misbehavior calls for immediate removal of the student from the classroom.

On page 49 are sample discipline hierarchies for elementary classrooms.

 Refer to *Assertive Discipline, Third Edition,* for an in-depth look at using corrective actions.

Sample Discipline Hierarchy for Grades K–3

First time a student breaks a rule:	Reminder
Second time:	5 minutes working away from group, near teacher
Third time:	10 minutes working away from group
Fourth time:	Call parents
Fifth time:	Send to principal
Severe clause:	Send to principal

Sample Discipline Hierarchy for Grades 4–6

First time a student breaks a rule:	Reminder
Second time:	10 minutes working away from group
Third time:	15 minutes working away from group, plus writing in behavior journal
Fourth time:	Call parents
Fifth time:	Send to principal
Severe clause:	Send to principal

Keeping Track of Corrective Actions With a Behavior Tracking Sheet

For your discipline hierarchy to be simple to use and easy to integrate into your teaching routine, you will need a system to keep track of student misbehavior and corrective actions accrued. You'll need to know at a glance the names of students who have received corrective actions, and where they are on the hierarchy. Keeping track doesn't have to be time-consuming and, most importantly, it doesn't have to interrupt your teaching.

On the following pages, you will see how to keep track of corrective actions using a "Behavior Tracking Sheet."

Here's how a Behavior Tracking Sheet works:

Make copies of the Behavior Tracking Sheet on page 51. Keep a sheet attached to a clipboard and close by you throughout the day and observe the following guidelines.

First time a student breaks a rule

Write down his or her name on the sheet and say, for example, "Manuel, the rule is 'Keep your hands to yourself.' This is a reminder."

> ➤ Circle the "Reminder" designation on the tracking sheet.

Second time a student breaks a rule

Speak quietly and calmly to the student, saying, for example, "Manuel, this is the second time you have misbehaved. You have chosen to sit by yourself in this chair near my desk."

➤ Circle the "2" on the tracking sheet, indicating that this is the second infraction of the day. The student moves his seat.

Third, fourth, or fifth time a student breaks a rule

If a student breaks a rule a third, fourth, or fifth time during the day, you must continue speaking quietly and calmly to the student, and continue recording the infractions on the tracking sheet. Make sure that the corrective actions are given according to your hierarchy. If your fourth action is "Call parents," be sure that you make that phone call. The success of your discipline plan depends upon your consistency.

Note: For some students, you may wish to jot down the rule broken. Then, if you notice a pattern of behavior developing, you will have documentation to help you solve that problem.

BEHAVIOR TRACKING SHEET

WEEK OF _____

Name	MONDAY	TUESDAY	WEDNESDAY	THURSDAY	FRIDAY
Manuel	Reminder 2 3 4 5	Reminder 2 3 4 5	Reminder 2 3 4 5	Reminder 2 3 4 5	Reminder 2 3 4 5
	Reminder 2 3 4 5	Reminder 2 3 4 5	Reminder 2 3 4 5	Reminder 2 3 4 5	Reminder 2 3 4 5
	Reminder 2 3 4 5	Reminder 2 3 4 5	Reminder 2 3 4 5	Reminder 2 3 4 5	Reminder 2 3 4 5
	Reminder 2 3 4 5	Reminder 2 3 4 5	Reminder 2 3 4 5	Reminder 2 3 4 5	Reminder 2 3 4 5
	Reminder 2 3 4 5	Reminder 2 3 4 5	Reminder 2 3 4 5	Reminder 2 3 4 5	Reminder 2 3 4 5
	Reminder 2 3 4 5	Reminder 2 3 4 5	Reminder 2 3 4 5	Reminder 2 3 4 5	Reminder 2 3 4 5
	Reminder 2 3 4 5	Reminder 2 3 4 5	Reminder 2 3 4 5	Reminder 2 3 4 5	Reminder 2 3 4 5
	Reminder 2 3 4 5	Reminder 2 3 4 5	Reminder 2 3 4 5	Reminder 2 3 4 5	Reminder 2 3 4 5
	Reminder 2 3 4 5	Reminder 2 3 4 5	Reminder 2 3 4 5	Reminder 2 3 4 5	Reminder 2 3 4 5
	Reminder 2 3 4 5	Reminder 2 3 4 5	Reminder 2 3 4 5	Reminder 2 3 4 5	Reminder 2 3 4 5
	Reminder 2 3 4 5	Reminder 2 3 4 5	Reminder 2 3 4 5	Reminder 2 3 4 5	Reminder 2 3 4 5
	Reminder 2 3 4 5	Reminder 2 3 4 5	Reminder 2 3 4 5	Reminder 2 3 4 5	Reminder 2 3 4 5
	Reminder 2 3 4 5	Reminder 2 3 4 5	Reminder 2 3 4 5	Reminder 2 3 4 5	Reminder 2 3 4 5
	Reminder 2 3 4 5	Reminder 2 3 4 5	Reminder 2 3 4 5	Reminder 2 3 4 5	Reminder 2 3 4 5
	Reminder 2 3 4 5	Reminder 2 3 4 5	Reminder 2 3 4 5	Reminder 2 3 4 5	Reminder 2 3 4 5

To the teacher: When a student receives a reminder, write the student's name on this tracking sheet. If a student breaks additional rules during the school day, circle each corrective action in the appropriate box. For example, if a student receives a reminder and chooses not to follow the rules again during the day, you would record: Reminder 2 3 4 5

51

BEHAVIOR TRACKING SHEET

WEEK OF _____

Name	MONDAY	TUESDAY	WEDNESDAY	THURSDAY	FRIDAY
	Reminder 2 3 4 5	Reminder 2 3 4 5	Reminder 2 3 4 5	Reminder 2 3 4 5	Reminder 2 3 4 5
	Reminder 2 3 4 5	Reminder 2 3 4 5	Reminder 2 3 4 5	Reminder 2 3 4 5	Reminder 2 3 4 5
	Reminder 2 3 4 5	Reminder 2 3 4 5	Reminder 2 3 4 5	Reminder 2 3 4 5	Reminder 2 3 4 5
	Reminder 2 3 4 5	Reminder 2 3 4 5	Reminder 2 3 4 5	Reminder 2 3 4 5	Reminder 2 3 4 5
	Reminder 2 3 4 5	Reminder 2 3 4 5	Reminder 2 3 4 5	Reminder 2 3 4 5	Reminder 2 3 4 5
	Reminder 2 3 4 5	Reminder 2 3 4 5	Reminder 2 3 4 5	Reminder 2 3 4 5	Reminder 2 3 4 5
	Reminder 2 3 4 5	Reminder 2 3 4 5	Reminder 2 3 4 5	Reminder 2 3 4 5	Reminder 2 3 4 5
	Reminder 2 3 4 5	Reminder 2 3 4 5	Reminder 2 3 4 5	Reminder 2 3 4 5	Reminder 2 3 4 5
	Reminder 2 3 4 5	Reminder 2 3 4 5	Reminder 2 3 4 5	Reminder 2 3 4 5	Reminder 2 3 4 5
	Reminder 2 3 4 5	Reminder 2 3 4 5	Reminder 2 3 4 5	Reminder 2 3 4 5	Reminder 2 3 4 5
	Reminder 2 3 4 5	Reminder 2 3 4 5	Reminder 2 3 4 5	Reminder 2 3 4 5	Reminder 2 3 4 5
	Reminder 2 3 4 5	Reminder 2 3 4 5	Reminder 2 3 4 5	Reminder 2 3 4 5	Reminder 2 3 4 5
	Reminder 2 3 4 5	Reminder 2 3 4 5	Reminder 2 3 4 5	Reminder 2 3 4 5	Reminder 2 3 4 5
	Reminder 2 3 4 5	Reminder 2 3 4 5	Reminder 2 3 4 5	Reminder 2 3 4 5	Reminder 2 3 4 5

To the teacher: When a student receives a reminder, write the student's name on this tracking sheet. If a student breaks additional rules during the school day, circle each corrective action in the appropriate box. For example, if a student receives a reminder and chooses not to follow the rules again during the day, you would record: Reminder ②③ 4 5

© 2002 Solution Tree

Suggested Corrective Actions

Here are some time-tested ideas that have been proven effective with elementary-age students.

Call time out—Remove a student from the group.

Removing a disruptive student from the group is not a new concept, but it is a very effective corrective action for elementary-age students. Designate a chair or table as the "time-out" area. Depending upon the age of the student, a trip to the time-out area could last from 5 to 10 minutes.

> *Note:* It's very important that students not be isolated from the rest of the class for long lengths of time. Keep your time within these limits.

While separated from the rest of the class, the student continues to do his or her classwork.

Assign writing in a behavior journal.

You want more from corrective actions than a student feeling contrite. You also want the student to learn from the experience. That's critical if a student is to learn to choose responsible behavior. You want him to think about his behavior, and how he can choose to behave differently in the future.

The following suggestion is appropriate for upper-elementary students.

When a student breaks a classroom rule, ask him write a "Behavior Journal" account of his misbehavior during recess, after class, or at home. This written account should include the following points:

1. The rule that was broken

    The rule I broke was "No hitting."

2. Why the student chose to break the rule or not follow the direction

    I hit Michael at recess because he was teasing me. He kept saying that my jacket was ugly.

3. What alternative action the student could have taken that would have been more appropriate

    Instead of hitting Michael, I could have ignored him. I could have walked away and played with someone else.

The student signs and dates the Behavior Journal sheet. The sheet should then be added to the student's documentation record. (It also can be sent home to parents as documentation of the student's misbehavior.)

Writing in the Behavior Journal helps students accept responsibility for their behavior. It also helps them think about choosing alternative behaviors in the future.

> *Note:* You may wish to use the Behavior Journal with your younger students, too. Ask students to dictate their entries to you or to an aide. Then use this time as an opportunity to discuss the student's behavior, and how he or she can make better choices in the future.

It's Your Turn

On page 54 you will find a reproducible Behavior Journal sheet. Make copies of this sheet and use it as part of your discipline hierarchy.

Write the corrective actions you choose on the poster on page 55.

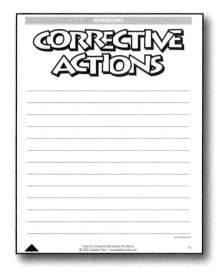

Behavior Journal

You have chosen to break a classroom rule. Please use this page to reflect on your own behavior. Remember, you are in control of what happens to you. You are responsible for your own actions.

Name: _____ Date: _____

This Is the Classroom Rule I Chose Not to Follow:

_____

_____

This Is What Happened:

_____

_____

_____

_____

This Is Why My Behavior Was Not Appropriate:

_____

_____

_____

_____

This Is What I Could Have Done Instead:

_____

_____

_____

_____

Your signature: _____ Date: _____

Assertive Discipline Elementary Workbook
© 2002 Solution Tree Press • solution-tree.com

CORRECTIVE ACTIONS

_____

_____

_____

_____

_____

_____

_____

_____

_____

_____

_____

Launching Your Classroom Discipline Plan

Your discipline plan is written. You've chosen the rules for your classroom, the supportive feedback you will give when students follow the rules, and the corrective actions you will take when your students choose to break the rules.

Ready to put it all into action?

Not quite.

The success of your classroom discipline plan depends on more than your planning and involvement alone. It also depends on the informed involvement of the others who will be affected by it: your students, your students' parents, and your administrator.

In this section of the *Assertive Discipline Elementary Workbook,* you will learn techniques for introducing your discipline plan. A selection of reproducibles is also included to help you plan and carry out an effective introduction.

Talk to Your Principal About Your Classroom Discipline Plan

Your principal is an integral part of your behavior management efforts. No matter how well-prepared you are, no matter how consistently and positively you use your discipline plan, you will still have one or two students that you will not be able to influence on your own. For these challenging students, you are going to need the help and cooperation of your principal. It is best to involve him or her at the very beginning.

Before you put your classroom discipline plan into effect, you must meet with your principal to discuss his or her role in your discipline plan.

Involving your principal is important for two reasons.

First, if you send a student to the office, according to the discipline hierarchy, your principal will want to know what steps you have already taken.

Second, so that you can follow up with a student, you will want to know exactly what action the principal will take when a student is sent to the office.

Present Your Plan

Make an appointment with your principal before school begins. Follow these guidelines for presenting your plan.

Explain your rationale for using a classroom discipline plan.

Begin by explaining why you are using a classroom discipline plan. Let your principal know that you are committed to having a classroom that is safe and orderly—a positive learning environment for your students, and a positive teaching environment for yourself. Explain that this is the reason you have established a classroom discipline plan with rules for behavior, supportive feedback when students follow the rules, and corrective actions when students choose to break the rules.

Emphasize that you will attempt to handle behavior problems on your own before you ever ask for the principal's help.

Your principal needs to know that before you send a student to the office, you first will take steps to respond to the student on your own.

Ask for Input

Have your principal read your plan. Ask for input to make sure that he or she is comfortable with all aspects of the plan. If the principal is not comfortable, ask for assistance in modifying the plan.

Discuss what the principal will do when a student is sent from your class to the office.

You need to know exactly what will happen when you send a student to the principal.

Many principals follow the hierarchy of consequences, such as:

First Time Sent to the Office

Counsel with the student, and suggest other ways he or she could have handled the situation.

Second Time Sent to the Office

Hold a parent conference to discuss the problem. Ask parents to support the school's efforts at home.

Third Time Sent to the Office

In-school suspension. The student does schoolwork outside of the regular classroom and in a closely supervised environment.

Severe

Counsel with the student, and hold a parent conference.

It is important for your principal to let you know what type of disciplinary action will be taken so you can follow up appropriately with the parents and the student. This can be accomplished by sending a note home or having a short meeting after school.

Discuss what will happen if the administrator is out of the building.

There may be times when you need to remove a disruptive student from your class and the principal is not in the building. Ask your principal what you should do in this circumstance.

Here are two alternatives:

1. Send the student to the school counselor.

2. Send the student to "time out" in another classroom.

With prior consent of another teacher, a disruptive student can be sent to a higher-grade classroom. When the student reaches the other classroom, he or she sits in a prearranged area away from the rest of the class. The student does not participate in the class activities and either sits quietly or does his or her own academic work.

Your administrator is an important part of your behavior management team. As such, the administrator needs to be informed in advance of his or her involvement and the support you expect. By introducing your discipline plan, you will assure the principal that you are prepared to handle student misbehavior on your own before asking for administrative assistance. And by mutually establishing what action your principal will take, you will help ensure that discipline problems will be handled in a fair and consistent manner by both of you.

Teach Your Classroom Discipline Plan to Your Students

A list of rules posted on your classroom wall is not enough to motivate students to always follow those rules. You must actively involve your students in the plan.

Teaching your classroom discipline plan to your students is as important as any lesson you will teach during the year. This lesson should take place the first day of school.

The lesson should cover the following points:

1. Explain why you need rules.
2. Teach the rules.
3. Check for understanding.
4. Explain how you will support students who follow the rules.
5. Explain why you need to use corrective actions when students do not follow the rules.
6. Explain the corrective actions.
7. Check for understanding.

Present Your Plan

Here are some suggestions for teaching your lesson.

1. Explain why you need rules.

First, make sure that all students understand what rules are and why they are needed. Talk about rules that students are already familiar with. Ask students to share comments about rules they have at home or have had in other classrooms:

"How many of you have rules at home?"

"What are some of the rules?"

"Why do you think your parents want you to follow rules at home?"

"What might happen in a classroom without rules? Would this be good for all students? Would it be harder for us to learn?"

2. Teach the rules.

Now you must clearly explain each of your classroom rules. Talk about why each rule is important and why you have chosen it. For example, the rule "Walk, don't run in the classroom" is important for safety reasons, and for moving from one activity to another calmly and quickly. If appropriate, role-play rules to aid understanding.

3. Check for understanding.

Now take the time to make sure that all students understand the rules you've taught. Ask students to repeat the rules in their own words. Then ask if there are any questions about the rules. Above all, make sure that students understand that these rules are in effect at all times—during all activities.

"Simone, is there ever a time when it's okay to run in the classroom?"

"Enrique, is it ever all right to hit another student?"

"Calvin, when I give a direction, what should you do?"

4. Explain how you will support students who follow the rules.

Supportive feedback is going to be the most important part of your classroom discipline plan. Tell your students that you know they can all be successful at following the rules of the classroom, and that it will be your pleasure to recognize and reward those students who follow the rules. Pique student enthusiasm and motivation by detailing the awards and privileges you will use:

> "See these good behavior bookmarks? I'll be giving these bookmarks to students who follow the rules."

5. Explain why you need to use corrective actions when students do not follow the rules.

Students need to understand that they are responsible for the behavioral choices they make. Explain your rationale:

> "Some of you may be wondering what will happen if you do not follow our rules. That's a fair question. After all, none of us is perfect. We all have trouble at times following the rules. Let's talk about this.

> Who can tell me what might happen at home if you break an important rule? Do your parents ever say 'No TV tonight' or 'You can't play after school'? Why do your parents do this? (Share responses.) Your parents do this to help you learn to be responsible for your actions.

> At school, I want to help you learn to behave responsibly too. When you choose to break a classroom rule, you need to learn that something will happen. Something you probably won't like very much."

6. Explain the corrective actions.

Tell students what you will do if they choose to misbehave once in a day (such as give a reminder), twice in a day, three times in a day, four times in a day, and five times in a day. Explain how you will keep track of their behavior:

> "See this clipboard? (Hold it up.) I'm going to keep it near me during the day. The first time you break a rule and disrupt the class, I will write your name on the clipboard. I'll also remind you of what the rules are. For example, if you are running in the classroom, all I will say to you is 'Juan, I want to remind you that the rule is "No running in the classroom."' If you are teasing your neighbor, I'll say 'Barbara, the rule is "No teasing." That's a reminder.'

> That's all I'll do.

> The reminder gives you a chance to choose better behavior. And I know you will choose better behavior.

> But if you do break this rule again, or any other rule during the day, I'll circle 2 on the chart. This means that you've broken a rule two times. And this means that you have chosen to sit for 5 minutes away from your group at a table near my desk. Being away from the group will give you time to calm down and think about your behavior."

Go through the rest of your discipline hierarchy in this manner, explaining each step. Afterward, take the time to emphasize your belief that the students can behave—and can act responsibly:

> "I know that all of you can follow our classroom rules. I know that all of you can make good decisions about how to behave."

7. Check for understanding.

It's important that all students understand the corrective actions you will use in the classroom. Ask if they have any questions.

Keep this in mind: The manner in which you present your discipline plan to your students will set the tone for your classroom for the entire year. Be positive! Communicate your high expectations. Emphasize to your students that they will all choose to follow the rules and enjoy the rewards of their good behavior. However, students must also understand that you will take action to correct their behavior if they choose to break a rule.

 Refer to *Assertive Discipline, Third Edition,* for additional sample scripts for teaching this lesson.

Teaching your classroom discipline plan is an important lesson, one that will impact your classroom environment for the rest of the year. Take the time to carefully plan the lesson. Use the "Lesson-Planning Worksheet" on pages 63 and 64 as you organize your lesson.

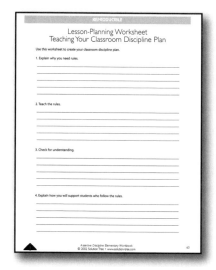

Lesson-Planning Worksheet:
Teaching Your Classroom Discipline Plan

Use this worksheet to create your classroom discipline plan.

1. Explain why you need rules.

_____

_____

_____

_____

_____

2. Teach the rules.

_____

_____

_____

_____

_____

3. Check for understanding.

_____

_____

_____

_____

_____

4. Explain how you will support students who follow the rules.

_____

_____

_____

_____

_____

5. Explain why you need to use corrective actions when students do not follow the rules.

_____

_____

_____

_____

_____

_____

_____

6. Explain the corrective actions.

_____

_____

_____

_____

_____

_____

_____

7. Check for understanding.

_____

_____

_____

_____

_____

_____

_____

Assertive Discipline Elementary Workbook
© 2002 Solution Tree Press • solution-tree.com

After You've Taught the Lesson . . .

Don't wait even one day to start reinforcing students for following your classroom rules. As soon as the lesson has been taught, look for opportunities to recognize students for good behavior and immediately begin reinforcing students who follow the rules.

Let students know that you notice and appreciate the good efforts they're making. Through your actions, let them know that you meant what you said about supporting their efforts:

"Jessica, good job following my directions today."

"Richard, you walked in the classroom quietly and began working immediately."

It's Your Turn

The following ideas will help support students' appropriate behavior at the start of the year.

Wear good behavior badges.

Encourage students' good behavior by wearing your own message of encouragement. These badges for teachers (see page 68) will serve as constant reminders to students of your behavioral expectations and will bring smiles to their faces as well. Use these badges in conjunction with the corresponding Desktop Behavior Charts.

Use desktop behavior charts.

The Desktop Behavior Charts on page 69 will help you recognize and reinforce students who follow the rules. When you spot a student exhibiting good behavior, stamp or add a sticker to his or her chart:

"Good job following directions, Carol. That's another stamp on your chart!"

These charts should be taped to each student's desk or placed in a special folder. When the chart, or designated portion thereof, is filled in, the student receives a reward. When completely filled, the chart is taken home to show parents.

Give out beginning-of-the-year awards.

Good habits start early in the year! The awards on pages 70–71 are specially designed to recognize students who follow the rules at the start of the year.

Post rules reminders.

Pages 72–74 have eye-catching posters of general rules that are commonly found in elementary classrooms. If these rules are part of your plan, ask students to color the posters and display them in the room. Depending on the age of the students, you may also pass them out for students to color and take home.

An open-ended bordered poster is also included to use for other rules of your own (see page 75), as well as a "School is cool when you follow the rules" poster (see page 76), which is applicable to any classroom.

Post your discipline plan.

Display the Rules, Supportive Feedback, and Corrective Actions posters (see pages 7, 39, and 55) in your classroom as an ever-present reminder of your classroom discipline plan. (This is important information for classroom visitors and new students, as well as substitutes.) Depending on their age, you may wish to give your students copies of these posters to keep.

And as the year proceeds . . .

Review your classroom rules frequently at the start of the year. Review them as needed as the year progresses. It's especially important to review classroom rules after vacations and on days when students are excited about special events (the day before a holiday, the first day of snow, a field trip day, Halloween, and so on).

More Great Ideas!

Here are some ideas that will help you teach and reinforce your classroom discipline plan.

Grades K–1: Read about rules.

Print one classroom rule on the lower part of a sheet of paper. Duplicate it and pass it out to students. Read the rule together. Talk once more about what the rule means. Ask students to draw a picture that goes with the rule. Do this for each of your classroom rules. When finished, staple the sheets together. As the year proceeds, use this booklet to help review and reinforce the rules.

Grades 2–4: Create a rules poster.

Have students copy the rules from the classroom discipline plan onto lined paper. Then pass out large sheets of construction paper. Have each student glue the list of rules on the construction paper poster and title it "Classroom Rules." Ask students to write in their own words why this plan will help them to learn to choose more responsible behavior in class.

Have students sign their posters, and you sign them, too. Students can take their posters home as reminders to parents, and themselves, of the classroom rules.

Grades 5–6: Create a classroom discipline folder.

Have students copy the classroom discipline plan as it is posted. Each student then places this copy in a Classroom Behavior folder. (The folder may also be used to keep copies of specific directions, as explained on pages 84–100.) After a day or two, give a short quiz on your classroom discipline plan. Tell students to use their copies of the plan to study.

Sample question might include the following:

> ➤ What are the four rules of our classroom? Write them down.

> ➤ How many times a day do you receive a reminder when you break a rule?

> ➤ What happens the second time you break a rule?

Assertive Discipline Elementary Workbook
© 2002 Solution Tree Press • solution-tree.com

_____ **is stuck on good behavior!**

_____ **is happy to follow the rules!**

_____ **loves to behave!**

© 2002 Solution Tree

To: _____
Student's name

Thanks for "pitching in" and getting this year off to a great start.

_____
Signed   Date

© 2002 Solution Tree

© 2002 Solution Tree

To: _____
Student's name

You're off to a "sunsational" start!

Thank you,

_____
Signed   Date

Assertive Discipline Elementary Workbook
© 2002 Solution Tree Press • solution-tree.com

_____
Student's name

is off to a "doggone" good start!

Thanks,

_____
Signed   Date

© 2002 Solution Tree

Who has "blasted off" to a great start?
_____ has!
Student's name

Thank you,

_____
Signed   Date

© 2002 Solution Tree

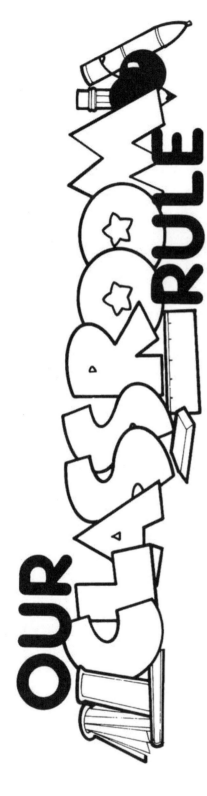

OUR CLASSROOM RULE

Follow directions.

Assertive Discipline Elementary Workbook
© 2002 Solution Tree Press • solution-tree.com

OUR CLASSROOM RULE

Keep hands, feet, and objects to yourself.

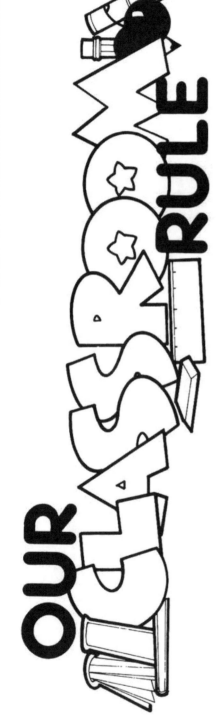

OUR CLASSROOM RULE

Do not leave the room without permission.

Assertive Discipline Elementary Workbook
© 2002 Solution Tree Press • solution-tree.com

School is cool when you follow the rules.

Assertive Discipline Elementary Workbook
© 2002 Solution Tree Press • solution-tree.com

Name _____ Class/Period _____

Name _____ Class/Period _____

Name _____ Class/Period _____

Name _____ Class/Period _____

Name _____ Class/Period _____

Name _____ Class/Period _____

Name _____ Class/Period _____

Name _____ Class/Period _____

Assertive Discipline Elementary Workbook
© 2002 Solution Tree Press • solution-tree.com

Share Your Classroom Discipline Plan With Parents and Substitutes

Present Your Plan to Parents

If parents are to become partners in their children's education, they must be well-informed about your classroom discipline plan. After all, contacting parents is part of your discipline hierarchy. You want parents to be involved when you need them. Parents, therefore, need to be informed about why you have a plan and your rationale for rules, supportive feedback, and corrective actions.

Give each student a copy of your discipline plan to take home to parents. In an accompanying letter, explain why a classroom discipline plan is important, and ask parents to go over the plan with their child, sign the plan, and send it back to you.

Tell your students:

> "Before you go home today, each of you will receive a copy of this letter to your parents. This letter explains our classroom discipline plan. I want all of you to talk with your parents about this plan. After you have talked about the plan, I want you and your parents to sign the bottom of the sheet. Please bring the tear-off portion back to me. I want all of your parents to know what I expect of you. And I want them to know that we will be working together to make sure this is a successful, happy year for all of you."

Your letter to parents should include the following:

➤ Your reason for having a classroom discipline plan

➤ A list of the rules, supportive feedback, and corrective actions that are included in your plan

➤ A message asking parents to support your discipline plan

➤ An invitation for parents to call you with any concerns they might wish to discuss

➤ A parent signature and comment sheet

 ## It's Your Turn

Look at the sample letter on page 80. This letter is only meant as a guide to writing your own letter. It is recommended that you use your own words.

Use the letterhead on page 81 to design your letter to parents. Make copies of the letterhead and run them through your computer's printer. You can scan the masthead into your computer, or design your own.

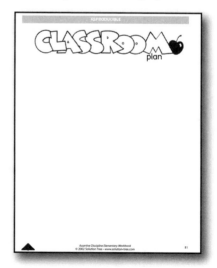

Prepare a Plan for Substitutes

You can't always be there every day. But you can make sure that your classroom continues to run smoothly—no matter who is in charge. To ensure consistent discipline in your classroom, even when you are not present, prepare a discipline plan for substitutes. Fill in your discipline plan on the "Substitute's Plan" sheet on page 82. Make sure that a copy is left in the office. Put another copy in your lesson plan book or tape it to the top of your desk.

The rules of your classroom must be in effect at all times. Therefore, it is important that any paraprofessionals or volunteers who work in your room understand the discipline plan and the role they are to play in its implementation. Take time to explain your plan to your support staff. Make it very clear how they are to respond to both positive and negative behavior.

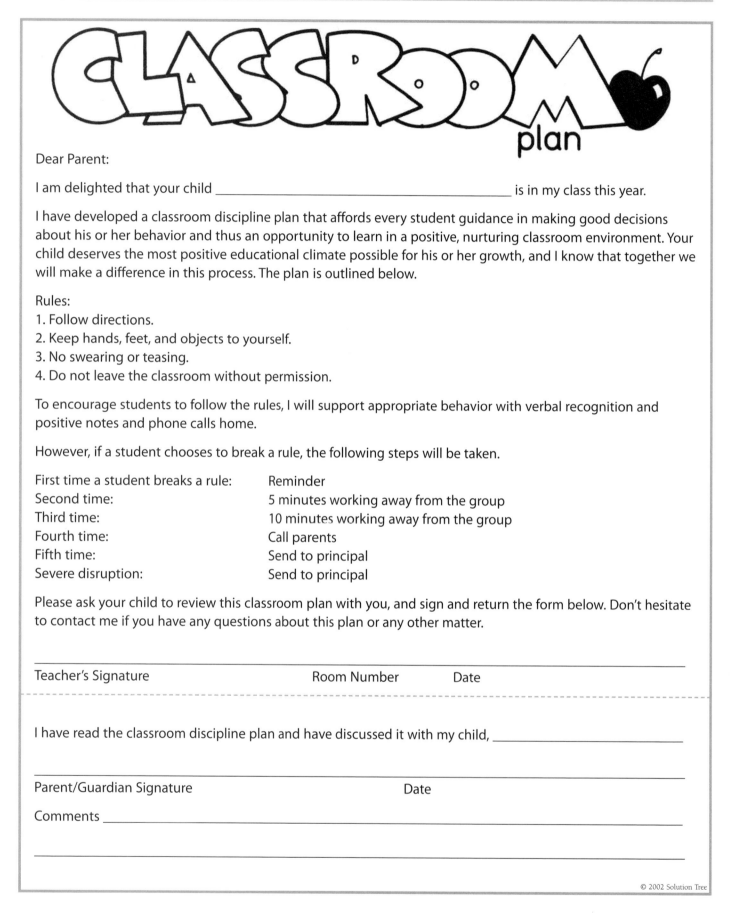

CLASSROOM plan

Dear Parent:

I am delighted that your child _____ is in my class this year.

I have developed a classroom discipline plan that affords every student guidance in making good decisions about his or her behavior and thus an opportunity to learn in a positive, nurturing classroom environment. Your child deserves the most positive educational climate possible for his or her growth, and I know that together we will make a difference in this process. The plan is outlined below.

Rules:
1. Follow directions.
2. Keep hands, feet, and objects to yourself.
3. No swearing or teasing.
4. Do not leave the classroom without permission.

To encourage students to follow the rules, I will support appropriate behavior with verbal recognition and positive notes and phone calls home.

However, if a student chooses to break a rule, the following steps will be taken.

First time a student breaks a rule:	Reminder
Second time:	5 minutes working away from the group
Third time:	10 minutes working away from the group
Fourth time:	Call parents
Fifth time:	Send to principal
Severe disruption:	Send to principal

Please ask your child to review this classroom plan with you, and sign and return the form below. Don't hesitate to contact me if you have any questions about this plan or any other matter.

_____

Teacher's Signature   Room Number   Date

- -

I have read the classroom discipline plan and have discussed it with my child, _____

_____

Parent/Guardian Signature   Date

Comments _____

_____

Assertive Discipline Elementary Workbook
© 2002 Solution Tree Press • solution-tree.com

Assertive Discipline Elementary Workbook
© 2002 Solution Tree Press • solution-tree.com

Substitute's Plan

From the desk of: _____

Dear Substitute:

Below are the guidelines for the discipline plan used in my classroom. Please follow them exactly, and leave me a list of students who break the rules and a list of students who behave properly.

Classroom Rules

1. _____
2. _____
3. _____
4. _____

Corrective Actions

When a student breaks a rule:

1st time_____

2nd time_____

3rd time_____

4th time_____

5th time_____

Severe Clause

If a student exhibits severe misbehavior such as fighting or open defiance, or uses vulgar language, please do the following:

_____

Rewards

Students who behave will be rewarded when I return with:

_____

_____

In addition, please offer plenty of positive recognition to students who follow the rules. They'll appreciate it! Thank you for following my classroom discipline plan.

Sincerely,

_____

Assertive Discipline Elementary Workbook
© 2002 Solution Tree Press • solution-tree.com

Teaching Responsible Behavior

Developing your classroom discipline plan and teaching this plan to your students are the first steps you take to help them choose the responsible behavior that will enable them to succeed in school.

The next step is to teach your students how to make responsible behavioral choices in all situations at school.

In this section of the *Assertive Discipline Elementary Workbook*, you will learn a variety of techniques that will help you motivate the majority of your students to behave appropriately.

Also included in this section is a wide selection of reproducibles that will help you implement these techniques.

Determine and Teach Specific Directions

Your classroom discipline plan lists the general rules of your classroom. As you have seen, these rules are in effect at all times.

The most important of these classroom rules is "Follow directions." This rule is included to ensure that students promptly follow any direction you might give during the day.

To comply with this rule, students must understand what each specific direction you give means. You can never assume that a roomful of young students will follow a direction in the same way. And you can certainly never assume that a roomful of students will follow a direction according to *your* expectations.

> ➤ Do your students know how you expect them to line up?
>
> ➤ Do they know how you expect them to transition from one activity to another?
>
> ➤ Do they know how you expect them to work together in groups?

There are many ways to go about following any direction. If you want all of your students to follow a direction in the same way, you must teach them. Right at the beginning of the year, you need to take time to teach your students exactly how you want them to behave in all classroom situations. You need to teach and reteach your expectations until every student knows how to line up, how to transition from one activity to another, and how to work in groups. Remember, the goal is for the students to succeed.

When Are Directions Needed?

The more time you spend at the beginning of the year teaching your specific directions, the less time you'll spend *repeating* them as the year goes by. Here's what to do:

First, identify the academic activities, routine procedures, and general policies for which specific directions are needed.

Next, determine the specific directions you want your students to follow for each activity and procedure you've identified.

Examples of Academic Activities

➤ Teacher-directed lessons

➤ Independent seatwork

➤ Working in pairs

➤ Working in small groups doing cooperative learning tasks

➤ Sustained silent reading

➤ Whole-group discussion

➤ Taking tests

➤ Working in centers

➤ Making presentations to the class

➤ Working with computers and other technology

Examples of Routine Procedures

➤ Entering the classroom

➤ Leaving the classroom

➤ Beginning the school day; ending the school day

➤ Collecting papers/homework

➤ Following an attention-getting signal

➤ Transitioning from one activity to another

➤ Lining up

➤ Taking attendance

➤ Getting/putting away equipment, books, and so on

➤ Observing emergency drills

Examples of General Policies

➤ Using the drinking fountain

➤ Using the pencil sharpener

➤ Using the restroom

➤ Care of desks, chairs, and other school property

➤ Use of computers

➤ Classroom interruptions (phone, visitors, and so on)

➤ Procedures for attending a school assembly

> Music, art, and P.E. teachers, and teachers who work in other special situations, have to come up with a list of the activities and procedures that apply to their students.

Special Procedures

➤ Putting music equipment away

➤ Putting sports equipment away

➤ Cleaning up after an art activity

The Difference Between Rules and Directions

➤ **Rules** are posted in your classroom, and are in effect at all times during the day.

➤ **Directions** are in effect for the duration of a specific activity.

➤ **Directions** may change based on the needs of the teacher and maturity level of the students.

It's Your Turn

Now think about a typical week in your own classroom. Start at the beginning of the school day on Monday and work your way through to the end of the day on Friday. Identify the academic activities, routine procedures, and general policies your students will be engaged in. Try not to leave anything out. Write all of these on a "Specific Directions List" (see page 86).

Specific Directions List

Use this worksheet to list all of the instructional settings, routine procedures, and general policies that occur during the school week.

Academic Activities

- _____
- _____
- _____
- _____
- _____
- _____

- _____
- _____
- _____
- _____
- _____
- _____

Routine Procedures

- _____
- _____
- _____
- _____
- _____
- _____

- _____
- _____
- _____
- _____
- _____
- _____

General Policies

- _____
- _____
- _____
- _____
- _____
- _____

- _____
- _____
- _____
- _____
- _____
- _____

Assertive Discipline Elementary Workbook
© 2002 Solution Tree Press • solution-tree.com

Determine Your Specific Directions

After you've listed all of the activities for which you need specific directions, it's time to decide on those directions. This is not as complicated as it might sound. When determining the specific directions you want your students to follow, use the following guidelines.

Keep it simple!

Choose a limited number of specific directions for each classroom activity.

Choose directions that are observable.

Your directions must be observable and easy for students to follow. Don't include vague directions such as "be good" or "behave appropriately."

Relate your directions to behaviors.

Explain how you want students to participate in the activity or procedures—what you expect them to do, and how you expect students to behave in order to be successful in the activity.

Examples of Specific Directions for an Elementary Classroom

Academic Activity: Teacher-directed lesson in front of the class

1. Clear your desks of everything but paper and pencil.

2. Eyes on me, or eyes on your paper. No talking while I'm talking.

3. Raise your hand and wait to be called upon to ask or answer a question. Don't shout out answers.

Academic Activity: Independent seatwork

1. Have all necessary books, paper, pencils, and other materials on your desk.

2. Begin working on your assignment as soon as you receive it.

3. No talking. Raise your hand to ask a question.

Routine Procedure: Entering the classroom

1. Walk into the room.

2. Go directly to your seat and sit down.

3. Take out your materials immediately.

4. No talking after the bell rings.

General Policies: Using the drinking fountain

1. Line up single-file and wait your turn.

2. Do not touch another student in line or at the fountain.

3. Do not spray or splash water at other students.

Specific Directions Worksheet

Write the specific directions for the classroom activities that apply to your own teaching situation. Some activities that generally take place in all classrooms have been added for you. Add to this list as needed.

Activity: Beginning the school day

1. _____
2. _____
3. _____

Activity: Going to recess

1. _____
2. _____
3. _____

Activity: Entering the classroom after recess

1. _____
2. _____
3. _____

Activity: Clean-up time

1. _____
2. _____
3. _____

Activity: Collecting homework

1. _____
2. _____
3. _____

Assertive Discipline Elementary Workbook
© 2002 Solution Tree Press • solution-tree.com

Now write directions for any other classroom activities you listed on page 86.

Activity: _____

1. _____
2. _____
3. _____

Activity: _____

1. _____
2. _____
3. _____

Activity: _____

1. _____
2. _____
3. _____

Activity: _____

1. _____
2. _____
3. _____

Activity: _____

1. _____
2. _____
3. _____

Activity: _____

1. _____
2. _____
3. _____

Activity: _____

1. _____

2. _____

3. _____

Activity: _____

1. _____

2. _____

3. _____

Activity: _____

1. _____

2. _____

3. _____

Activity: _____

1. _____

2. _____

3. _____

Activity: _____

1. _____

2. _____

3. _____

Activity: _____

1. _____

2. _____

3. _____

Assertive Discipline Elementary Workbook
© 2002 Solution Tree Press • solution-tree.com

Teach Your Specific Directions

Once you've determined your specific directions, your goal in teaching them is not to simply pass along instructions, but to make this process a learning experience for students as well.

Teach students *why* your directions are important to everyone's well-being. When students understand the reason behind your directions, they'll be much more likely to follow them.

Why teach specific directions with such care?

Here are two good reasons:

1. Teaching specific directions ensures that behavior problems will be reduced throughout the day.

2. Teaching specific directions ensures greater academic success. Students know how to be successful during each activity. Less time is wasted during transitions.

As with any successful lesson, preparation is vital to meeting your objectives. The lesson sequence that follows highlights points you'll want to include in your own specific directions lessons. Use this as a guideline for developing a lesson for any specific direction. Keep in mind that your own lessons will differ, based on the age of your students and the direction you are teaching, but the focus on **explanation, teaching,** and **checking for understanding** remains the same.

With younger students in **grades K–3**, you will want to spend plenty of time teaching and reinforcing each specific direction lesson. Give students the opportunity to role-play the directions, and give them ample opportunity to follow the directions after the lesson is given. Reteach and reinforce often. Use pictures or other visual clues to help reinforce the directions.

Students in **grades 4–6** want to understand the reasons behind the directions they are expected to follow. Explain why they need to follow the directions and what the benefit will be to them and the other students.

A sample lesson sequence for teaching specific directions follows.

1. Explain the rationale for the directions.

Students need to understand why your directions are important. Explain why they need to follow these directions and what the benefit will be to them and to other students.

"Several times a day, I will give you the direction to line up at the door. You'll hear this direction every day before recess, before lunchtime, and before P.E. So that we can all leave the classroom safely and quickly, it's important to follow directions when you line up."

2. Involve the students by asking questions.

Students will follow your directions more readily if you involve them in a discussion that rationally addresses your concerns.

> "Why do you think I want you to follow certain directions when you line up at the door? What could happen if we had no directions to follow at all? Do you think we'd all do the same thing?

> Jenny, what would you do? Would you put your books away before you line up?

> Sam, would you stop on the way to take a drink of water?

> Bill, would you get your jacket first?

> How many of you would rush to be first?

> Now, what could happen if some of you rushed to get a drink of water, some of you raced to the door, some of you went to get your jackets, and some of you just talked at your desks?

> I think you can see why it's a good idea for all of us to be doing the same thing at the same time."

3. Teach the specific directions.

Now teach the students the directions they are to follow:

> "All right, these are the directions we are going to follow when it's time to line up at the door. When I say 'Class, line up at the door,' this is what I expect you to do: First, I want you to put all of your books, pencils, paper, and any other materials into your desk. Second, I want you to stand and quietly push your chair under your desk. And third, I want you to walk quietly, without talking, to the door and line up."

4. Check for understanding.

Check for understanding by asking students to restate the directions. Then reinforce the directions further by writing them on the board. (With K–1 students, you might choose to show a poster that graphically teaches the directions.) Ask:

> "All right, who can raise their hand and tell me what you will do first when I give the direction to line up at the door?"

Next, ask students to role-play the directions:

> "Let's practice what you've just learned. When I give the direction, I want you all to follow the directions you've learned and line up at the door. Ready? Class, please line up at the door."

Immediately begin to recognize those students who are following the directions:

> "Mary has put her books away and is lining up. Kyle is walking quietly to the door. Jeff is putting his chair under his desk. Good work!"

> "Now, does anyone have any questions about how to line up at the door?"

After You've Taught a Specific Directions Lesson . . .

Immediately follow up any specific directions lesson with the activity or procedure that has just been taught. Be sure to reinforce students who follow the directions appropriately, and give reminders (or reteach if necessary) to those students who don't.

First 2 weeks

Review directions each time the class engages in the activity.

First month

Review directions each Monday as a reminder and refresher for the week to come.

Remainder of year

Review directions as needed. It is especially important to review directions after a vacation, or on special days when students are excited (such as field trip day, the day before vacation, Halloween, and so on).

It's Your Turn

Here are some ideas that will help you teach specific directions to your students.

Plan your lessons.

Use the "Lesson Plan for Teaching Specific Directions" on pages 94–95 to plan the lessons you will teach. Run off plenty of copies and use them to write down questions you want to ask your students during the lesson, points you want to make, and other reminders to yourself.

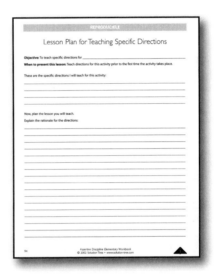

Lesson Plan for Teaching Specific Directions

Objective: To teach specific directions for _____

When to present this lesson: Teach directions for this activity prior to the first time the activity takes place.

These are the specific directions I will teach for this activity:

_____

_____

_____

_____

Now, plan the lesson you will teach.

Explain the rationale for the directions:

_____

_____

_____

_____

_____

_____

_____

_____

_____

_____

_____

_____

_____

_____

_____

_____

Assertive Discipline Elementary Workbook
© 2002 Solution Tree Press • solution-tree.com

Involve the students by asking questions:

_____

_____

_____

_____

_____

_____

_____

Teach the specific directions:

_____

_____

_____

_____

_____

_____

_____

_____

Check for understanding:

_____

_____

_____

_____

Notes on the lesson:

_____

_____

_____

_____

_____

_____

Post your directions.

Visual reminders can often help students remember directions. Use the open-ended "Directions for_____" poster on page 97 to create handy reminders of your directions.

Recognize students who follow directions.

The reproducible awards on pages 98–100 will help you recognize students who follow directions.

Create a classroom directions binder.

As new students enter your class throughout the year, they too will need to learn your specific directions. This idea (for grades 2 and up) can ease their transition and involve peers in the teaching process.

Use the open-ended "Directions for _____" worksheet on page 97 to create directions sheets for different activities.

Organize these sheets into a loose-leaf binder. Ask a student to decorate a cover sheet to create an inviting notebook that will be part of your classroom all year long. When a new student joins the class, assign him or her a buddy. It will be the responsibility of the buddy to go through the binder with the new student and explain each of these directions.

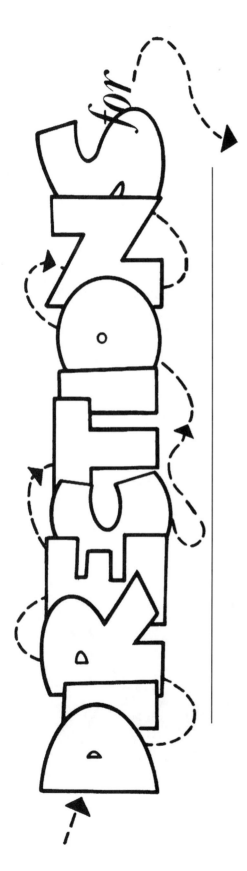

Congratulations, _____!
Student's name

You were "caught" following directions!

Good Job!

_____
Signed   Date

To: _____
Student's name

Thanks for following directions!

_____
Signed   Date

To: _____
Student's name

I'd like to say a few words about the way you behave in class . . .

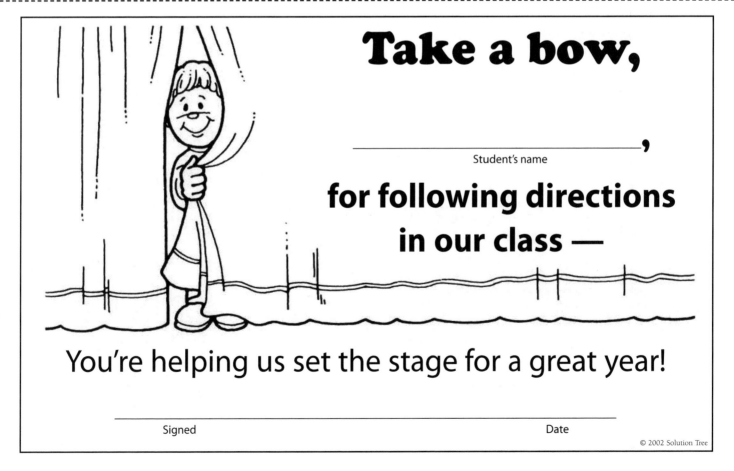

TERRIFIC!

SUPER!

GOOD JOB!

_____
Signed   Date

© 2002 Solution Tree

Take a bow,

_____,
Student's name

for following directions in our class —

You're helping us set the stage for a great year!

_____
Signed   Date

© 2002 Solution Tree

_____
Student's name

was "caught" following directions.

_____
Signed   Date

_____
Student's name

was "caught" following directions.

_____
Signed   Date

© 2002 Solution Tree

Way to go,

_____!
Student's name

You were "caught" following directions.

_____
Signed

© 2002 Solution Tree

_____
Student's name

was "caught" following directions.

_____
Signed   Date

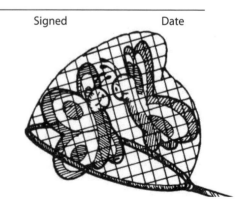

© 2002 Solution Tree

Assertive Discipline Elementary Workbook
© 2002 Solution Tree Press • solution-tree.com

Use Supportive Feedback to Motivate Students to Behave

Once you've taught your students directions for all classroom activities, your goal is to help them be successful in following those directions.

Supportive feedback is the most effective way to achieve this goal.

There are a variety of techniques that you can use to motivate students to choose appropriate behavior and then to *continue* that behavior.

These techniques are:

1. Behavioral narration

2. Verbal recognition

3. Scanning

4. Circulating the classroom

On the following pages, you will learn how to use each of these techniques throughout the day—while you teach, and while you are involved in any classroom activity.

Keep Assertive Discipline in Action! Cue Cards as Reminders

Cue cards are a quick and easy way to keep Assertive Discipline techniques close at hand and in your mind. All of the supportive feedback techniques listed in this chapter, and other behavior management techniques included in upcoming chapters, have been organized into easy-to-use "Assertive Discipline in Action!" Cue Cards.

These reproducible cue cards give you portable, to-the-point references for successfully handling both appropriate and inappropriate classroom behavior.

Follow these guidelines for using cue cards.

Read Them

Read each cue card. Think about how you can use each of these techniques in the day-to-day routine of your classroom.

Keep Them

Laminate the cue cards and then tuck them into the back of your lesson plan book for easy reference. From time to time, review the techniques and make sure you are using them effectively and consistently.

Share Them

Give a set of cue cards to your classroom aide or to parent volunteers. Encourage them to read the cards and use the techniques with students.

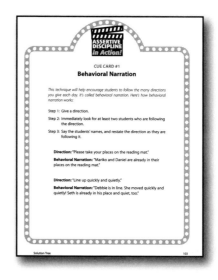

Cue Card #1

Behavioral Narration

This technique will help encourage students to follow the many directions you give each day. It's called behavioral narration. Here's how behavioral narration works:

Step 1: Give a direction.

Step 2: Immediately look for at least two students who are following the direction.

Step 3: Say the students' names, and restate the direction as they are following it.

Direction: "Please take your places on the reading mat."

Behavioral Narration: "Mariko and Daniel are already in their places on the reading mat."

Direction: "Line up quickly and quietly."

Behavioral Narration: "Debbie is in line. She moved quickly and quietly! Seth is already in his place and quiet, too."

© 2002 Solution Tree

Cue Card #1 (BACK)

Frequency of Behavioral Narration

At the beginning of the year, you will be placing a heavy emphasis on teaching students how to behave and how to follow your classroom rules. Thus, at the beginning of the year, you will use behavioral narration and other means of support much more frequently than you will once your students learn what you need them to do in each classroom situation. Remember, one of the goals of using supportive feedback is to start strong, then gradually decrease the frequency.

Weeks 1–2:   Use behavioral narration every time you give a direction. Don't worry about overdoing it.

Weeks 2–4:   Use behavioral narration every third time you give a direction.

After first month: Use behavioral narration every fourth or fifth time you give a direction. Maintain this frequency level throughout the year.

Behavioral narration is a positive advantage for you and your students!

You give hundreds of directions in a week. Each time you give a direction, you have a ready-made opportunity to acknowledge students. When you get into the habit of using this technique, you will make many more positive than negative statements to students.

© 2002 Solution Tree

Assertive Discipline Elementary Workbook
© 2002 Solution Tree Press • solution-tree.com

Cue Card #2

Verbal Recognition

An effective way to encourage students to continue their appropriate behavior is to continually monitor the class—even while teaching—and provide frequent verbal recognition to those students who are on task. Keep these guidelines in mind.

Verbal recognition is personal.

Always include the student's name. A statement like "Thank you for working quietly" is not as meaningful as "Kara and Jessica, you are tackling the assignment in soft voices without disturbing those around you. Your cooperation is much appreciated."

Verbal recognition must be genuine.

To be convincing to students, to show that you really mean what you say, be genuinely appreciative of their appropriate behavior.

Verbal recognition is descriptive and specific.

When acknowledging students, be specific. That way, students will know exactly what they did to deserve the recognition and will be more likely to repeat those behaviors.

Descriptive Verbal Recognition:	Vague Verbal Recognition:
"Shauntia is lining up for recess. Thanks, Shauntia."	"You're so good, Shauntia."
"You did a great job on your spelling test, Mark."	"Nice job, Mark."
"Thank you for putting the books away, Sara."	"I like the way you're helping, Sara."

© 2002 Solution Tree

Cue Card #3

Scanning

The scanning technique for motivating students to stay on task is useful when you are working with a small group of students or an individual student while the rest of the class works independently. Here's how to use the scanning technique.

Step 1: When you are working with a small group, look up every few minutes and scan the students who are working independently.

Step 2: As you notice students who are working appropriately, take a moment to recognize their good behavior.

"Robert is working quietly on his social studies assignment. Keep up the good work, Robert."

Step 3: The student will appreciate the recognition and continue working independently. Other students will get the message that you are aware of what's going on in the room and will be motivated to stay on task.

Assertive Discipline Elementary Workbook
© 2002 Solution Tree Press • solution-tree.com

Cue Card #4

Circulating the Classroom

While students are working independently, circulate the room and give verbal recognition. One-on-one, you can let a student know that you recognize his or her appropriate behavior. This acknowledgment is given quietly—a special message from the teacher to the student.

"Mike, you remained focused on your science assignment for the entire lesson. You're going to finish the whole assignment!"

"Jocelyn, you've been very cooperative today. You are doing a great job getting along with everyone."

There is no need to ever phase out this technique. Each time you circulate the classroom, you have an opportunity to show your students that you care and that you notice their good efforts.

Redirect Nondisruptive Off-Task Behavior

By teaching your rules and specific directions and by providing consistent positive support to your students, you can eliminate the majority of problems before they even begin.

Experience has perhaps shown you, however, that there will still be students who behave inappropriately. This behavior can take two forms: disruptive off-task behavior and nondisruptive off-task behavior.

Disruptive Off-Task Behaviors

➤ Shouting out in class

➤ Throwing paper or other objects

➤ Pushing or shoving another student

➤ Running in the classroom

➤ Talking back to the teacher

Nondisruptive Off-Task Behaviors

➤ Looking out the window

➤ Reading instead of listening

➤ Doodling instead of working

➤ Daydreaming

You will learn about disruptive off-task behavior and how to respond to it on pages 114–115. Now we will focus on how to respond to nondisruptive off-task behavior—behavior in which a student is not disrupting others, but is not paying attention or following directions, either.

How to Redirect

As any teacher knows, students often fall into nondisruptive off-task behavior. They often lose focus and become inattentive to the work going on in class. It doesn't take much for a first grader to start doodling on his paper, or for a fifth grader to lose interest in her class and begin to stare out the window.

The teacher's responsibility is to guide the student back into learning.

Here's what you *don't* want to do.

1. Ignore the behavior.

2. Respond immediately with a corrective action.

Ignoring the behavior doesn't get the student back on task, and therefore the student isn't participating or learning.

Using a corrective action, in many cases, is an overreaction to a simple lapse of attention.

Here's what you want to do.

Gently, and with caring guidance, give the student an opportunity to get back on task.

✎ It's Your Turn

The Assertive Discipline in Action! Cue Cards on pages 110–113 contain four techniques that will help you redirect a student's nondisruptive off-task behavior *while* you teach:

1. The "Look"

2. Physical Proximity

3. Mention Student's Name

4. Proximity Praise

Read each technique and imagine how you can use it throughout the day to nudge students back into your lessons. Reproduce these cue cards, laminate them, and keep them nearby for easy and frequent review.

Once a Student Is Back on Track . . .

As soon as a student is back on task, take advantage of the opportunity to verbally recognize his or her behavior. Let the student know that paying attention in class earns your positive attention.

How often do you redirect?

How many times should you redirect students before you start giving consequences? Obviously, you can't go on redirecting a student over and over within a day. At some point, you may have to correct the student's actions.

Here's a rule of thumb.

When you find yourself having to redirect a student three times a day, you can assume that the student is not receiving enough structure to help control his or her behavior. In these situations, turn to your discipline hierarchy and issue a reminder.

If the off-task behavior still continues, you may need to proceed to a further step on your discipline hierarchy.

> *Note:* If the off-task behavior still seems out of character for a student, perhaps there's something wrong. Before turning to your hierarchy, talk to the student and ask, for example, "It seems like it's hard for you to pay attention in class today. Would you like to talk about it?" Always remember that your own good judgment is your most valuable guide in assessing student behavior.

Cue Card #5

The "Look"

Just giving a look that says "I'm aware of and disapprove of your behavior" is an effective way of redirecting nondisruptive off-task behavior. Here's how this technique works.

Instead of reading her book, Jessica is rocking back and forth in her seat. When the teacher notices Jessica's off-task behavior, he makes direct eye contact with the student and looks at her with a firm, calm look on his face. The teacher maintains this eye contact until Jessica puts all four legs of her chair on the floor and begins to read her book.

© 2002 Solution Tree

Assertive Discipline Elementary Workbook
© 2002 Solution Tree Press • solution-tree.com

Cue Card #6

Physical Proximity

Sometimes you don't even have to say a word to redirect a student back on task. Simply walk over and stand close by the student. The student will know why you've arrived at his or her side and will respond. Here's an example of physical proximity at work.

While reading a story to the class, the teacher notices that Danny has put his head down on his desk and tuned out. Continuing to read, the teacher walks over to Danny's desk and stands there while she proceeds with the story. Danny becomes aware of her presence, lifts his head, and starts paying attention.

© 2002 Solution Tree

Cue Card #7

Mention Student's Name

Just mentioning the off-task student's name while you are teaching a lesson may be enough to redirect his or her attention back on task. Here's an example of a teacher using this technique.

While at the board, the teacher notices that Rosa and Michael are off task and not paying attention. The teacher, in a matter-of-fact manner, continues the lesson, saying, "I want all of you, including Rosa and Michael, to come up with the answer to this problem." As soon as their names are mentioned, Rosa and Michael immediately begin paying attention.

© 2002 Solution Tree

Assertive Discipline Elementary Workbook
© 2002 Solution Tree Press • solution-tree.com

Cue Card #8

Proximity Praise

An effective way to redirect a nondisruptive off-task student back on task is to focus on the appropriate behavior of those students around him or her. Here's an example of a teacher using proximity praise.

The entire class, with the exception of Jama, is working independently on their assignments. Rather than doing her assignment, Jama is doodling in her notebook. On either side of Jama, Colleen and Jeff are both doing their work. Wanting to get Jama on task, the teacher says, "Colleen and Jeff are following directions and working independently on their math assignments. Excellent job."

As the teacher expects, Jama looks around, notices what is going on, and gets back to work.

This technique is doubly effective. Off-task students are motivated to get back on task, and students who are on task receive well-deserved recognition.

© 2002 Solution Tree

Implement Corrective Actions

The previous techniques in this book will work to keep most students on task. However, when students disrupt and keep you from teaching or other students from learning, you will have to follow through with the corrective actions you have proactively planned.

On page 48, you learned to develop a discipline hierarchy as part of your classroom discipline plan. How you use the hierarchy will determine its success in helping you motivate students to choose responsible behavior.

> *Remember:* Students need to learn that corrective actions are a natural outcome of misbehavior. The key is not the corrective action itself, but the inevitability that an action will be taken each time a rule is broken or a direction is not followed. Not sometimes, not every now and then, but every single time.

To successfully manage a classroom, there must be a balance between giving supportive feedback and providing corrective actions. Students will not respect your supportive feedback unless it is backed up with firm limits.

Help Students Choose Responsible Behavior

Follow these guidelines to ensure that your use of corrective actions will help students choose responsible behavior.

1. Provide corrective actions in a calm, matter-of-fact manner.

One of the benefits of a discipline hierarchy is that you always know how you will react to student misbehavior. Because you've planned how to respond to misbehavior, you will be able to follow through calmly, without anger, and with the assuredness that the corrective action is both appropriate and fair. For example, say:

> "Beverly, this is the second time I've had to speak to you about running in the classroom. You have chosen to go to work away from the group for five minutes."

2. Be consistent—Provide a corrective action every time a student chooses to disrupt.

As noted previously, it is the consistency of using corrective actions that is the key to their effectiveness.

3. After correcting a student's behavior, find the first opportunity you can to recognize positive behavior.

After a student has been disruptive and has received a corrective action, teachers often begin to focus on that student's negative behavior—just waiting for that student to act up again. This may be a natural response, but it does little to encourage a student to choose more appropriate behavior.

Don't look for negative behavior. Instead, take the first opportunity to recognize the student's appropriate behavior.

4. Provide an "escape mechanism" for students who are upset and want to talk about what happened.

After receiving a corrective action, students will often want you to stop what you are doing and listen to their side of the story.

The following "escape mechanism" will let students defuse their anger and "get something off their chest," without disrupting the rest of the class:

> ➤ Ask the student to write you a note that you will discuss with him or her after class or when you have a break in the lesson.

> ➤ Use a notebook to record misbehavior that allows space for students to write their comments.

> ➤ Have students keep a daily journal or diary in which they can record any comments.

5. When a student continuously disrupts, "move in."

There may be times when a student will continue to disrupt even after he or she has been given a reminder and a corrective action. In these situations, a technique called "moving in" (see Cue Card #9 on page 116) will often effectively stop disruptive behavior.

Keep in mind that by calmly and consistently implementing your discipline plan, you will help most students choose responsible behavior in your classroom. In spite of these efforts, however, there are going to be some cases in which students will challenge your authority and confront you. When a student tries to manipulate you or argue with you, you must stay in charge and refocus the conversation. Refer to the refocusing technique on Cue Card #10 (see page 117) for specific guidelines.

 Refer to *Assertive Discipline, Third Edition*, for additional examples of effective uses of corrective actions.

Cue Card #9

"Moving In"

Many times physical proximity is all that is needed to help calm down a student and stop the disruptive behavior. Here's an effective technique to use when a student is being disruptive in class.

Step 1: Move close to the student.

Walk over to the student. Get close. Show your concern and, in a quiet, firm manner, let the student know that his or her behavior is inappropriate.

Step 2: In a caring manner, remind the student of the corrective actions taken so far, and what will happen next if the misbehavior continues.

"Monica, I am concerned that your behavior today is going to result in some corrective actions that you really don't want. You've been doing such a good job all week. I'm proud of the work you've done and I'd like to see it continue. Now, you've disrupted class three times today. One more disruption and I will be calling your parents tonight. Do you understand?"

Assertive Discipline Elementary Workbook
© 2002 Solution Tree Press • solution-tree.com

CUE CARD #10

Refocusing an Argumentative Conversation

When a student starts arguing with you, you must stay in charge. Do not get involved in an argument. Do not let the student pull you into a pointless exchange. Instead, stay in control, refocus the conversation, and help get the student back on task. Here's what to do:

- Stay calm.

- State what you want: "I want you to sit down and do your assignment."

- State your understanding for the child.

- Repeat this statement a maximum of three times. If the student still argues, let her know that she may be choosing to receive a corrective action.

Here's an example of a teacher using the refocusing technique with a disruptive student:

Teacher: *(Calmly but firmly)* Janis, I want you to sit down and get to work on your assignment.

Janis: Why do I always have to sit down? Katy gets to clean up the reading area. That's not fair.

Teacher: I understand, Janis, but I want you to sit down and start your work.

Janis: But I want to help Katy put away books. I don't want to sit down.

Teacher: Janis, I see that you're upset, but sit down and begin your work.

Janis: Everyone else always gets to help.

Teacher: Janis, if you don't get to work immediately, you and I will call your mother during recess. The choice is yours.

Working With Difficult Students

Consistent use of the classroom management skills presented in the first part of this workbook will enable most teachers to teach 90 to 95 percent of their students to choose responsible behavior.

The remaining 5 to 10 percent—the difficult students you sometimes encounter—are the focus of this section. This section covers four ways to work successfully with difficult students:

1. Build positive relationships.

2. Conduct one-on-one problem-solving conferences.

3. Develop an individualized behavior plan.

4. Gain support from parents and administrators.

Build Positive Relationships

Make a special effort to establish positive relationships with difficult students—relationships that demonstrate your care and commitment to their success and well-being. Show these students that you care about them as unique individuals and that you are deeply concerned about their behavior.

When working with difficult students, you must go beyond the guidelines of your classroom discipline plan. Use special approaches and activities that enable you to reach out to those students on an individual basis to build a strong, positive relationship.

 **It's Your Turn**

The following pages contain ideas for fostering and building positive relationships with difficult students: a "Student Interest Inventory," a "Teacher Interest Inventory," and an Assertive Discipline in Action! Cue Card detailing effective techniques to use with difficult students.

Discover your students' interests.

In order to establish personal relationships with your students, you need to learn about their likes and dislikes, interests, and goals. A Student Interest Inventory, taken at the beginning of the year, is a great way to learn more about each student. Explain to your students that this inventory will help you become better acquainted with each student. Make this inventory (see page 122) the first homework assignment of the year. Keep a supply of Student Interest Inventories on hand throughout the year to give to transfer students entering your classroom. The information you gather from this inventory could be the building blocks of a positive relationship.

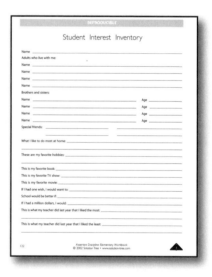

Turnabout is fair play!

Don't forget, students will want to know something about you, too. Create a Teacher Interest Inventory detailing your likes and dislikes, interests, and goals. Distribute a copy of the completed inventory to each student. Encourage students to discuss the inventory with you. Use the reproducible on page 123. (For younger students, share this information orally, followed by a question-and-answer period.)

Reach out.

Build strong, positive relationships with difficult students by incorporating the simple yet effective techniques found on Assertive Discipline in Action! Cue Card #11 (see page 124) into your daily routine. Keep this cue card handy as a reminder of the many ways you can make positive contact with all students, especially difficult ones, throughout the day. While many of the ideas are suitable for all of your students, it is especially important to reach out to the most challenging ones. Those students may have come to your class with negative attitudes and distrust for adults. You will have to make a concerted effort to reach out to them to show you care.

Student Interest Inventory

Name _____

Adults who live with me:

Name _____

Name _____

Name _____

Name _____

Brothers and sisters:

Name _____ Age _____

Name _____ Age _____

Name _____ Age _____

Name _____ Age _____

Special friends: _____ _____

_____ _____

What I like to do most at home: _____

_____

These are my favorite hobbies: _____

_____

This is my favorite book: _____

This is my favorite TV show: _____

This is my favorite movie: _____

If I had one wish, I would want to: _____

School would be better if: _____

If I had a million dollars, I would: _____

This is what my teacher did last year that I liked the most: _____

_____

This is what my teacher did last year that I liked the least: _____

_____

Assertive Discipline Elementary Workbook
© 2002 Solution Tree Press • solution-tree.com

Teacher Interest Inventory

Name _____

Family (optional):

Spouse _____

Children (ages) _____

Brothers and sisters _____

What I like to do most at home: _____

_____

_____

These are my favorite hobbies:_____

_____

_____

This is my favorite book: _____

This is my favorite TV show: _____

This is my favorite movie: _____

This is my favorite performer: _____

If I had one wish, I would want to: _____

_____

_____

If I had a million dollars, I would: _____

_____

_____

What I like best about teaching: _____

_____

_____

Why I became a teacher: _____

_____

_____

Cue Card #11

© 2002 Solution Tree

Ideas for Building Positive Relationships

Greet your students at the door.

Start each day with a smile and a personal greeting—for each and every student. Stand at the door as your students enter the room and greet each student by name. "Good morning, Jamal. Nice to see you, Rebecca. Hi, George." This is an especially effective way to make personal, positive contact with those students who need individual attention and caring words.

Spend a few special minutes with students who need your one-on-one attention.

The most precious and valuable gift you can give difficult students is your undivided attention. Take a few minutes during class, at recess, during lunch, or after school to talk to the student. Share information about yourself. Inquire about the student's feelings and concerns. Let that student know that you are there to offer assistance, understanding, and a sympathetic ear when necessary.

Make a phone call after a difficult day.

End a difficult day on a positive note by phoning a student with a positive message about tomorrow. Discuss any difficulties that occurred during the day. Get student input. Most important, the phone call should

emphasize your confidence that these problems can be worked through and that tomorrow both of you can start fresh.

Make a positive phone call when a student has had a good day.

What better way to let a student know that he or she is on the right track than by making a quick phone call to offer some well-earned words of praise? If the student isn't home, share the good news with parents and have them deliver the positive message later.

Make get-well calls.

When a student is ill, pick up the phone and call to find out how the child is feeling. Both parents and student will appreciate your caring and concern.

Recognize a student's strengths and achievements, both academic and nonacademic.

Look for areas in which a student shows particular strength (sports, music, art). Besides verbally recognizing the student's ability, find opportunities to engage the student to use his or her strength. (Invite the student to participate in a special school event. Suggest that the student take part in designing a school mural.)

Assertive Discipline Elementary Workbook
© 2002 Solution Tree Press • solution-tree.com

Conduct One-on-One Problem-Solving Conferences

A one-on-one problem-solving conference is a meeting between you and a student to discuss a specific behavior problem. The goal of this conference is not to punish but to listen to the student and give caring and firm guidance. This conference should be looked upon as a cooperative effort on the student's behalf.

When Is a One-on-One Conference Needed?

Ask yourself, "If this were my child, would I want her teacher to sit down and work with her to improve her behavior? Would I want her teacher to take time and interest to show my child options?"

If the answer is yes, then it is time to meet with the student.

Grades K–3

Young students are very concrete. Your discussion must be quite specific about how the child should behave. You may actually want to role-play the behaviors you want the student to engage in to ensure that he or she understands what you mean.

Grades 4–6

At this age, students do not want to be told what to do. They want to feel they have a say in how they choose to behave. Whenever possible, involve the student in discussing how the student should change his or her behavior.

Conducting the Conference

Keep these guidelines in mind when conducting a one-on-one problem-solving conference.

1. Show empathy and concern.

First and foremost, let the student know that you are concerned and that you care about her. Let the student know that you are meeting not to punish but to help and offer guidance.

2. Question the student to find out why there is a problem.

Don't assume you know why the student is misbehaving. Ask questions:

"Did something happen to you today to get you so upset?"

"Are other students bothering you?"

"Do you have trouble seeing the board?"

"Is the work too difficult for you?"

"Is there something happening at home or in your neighborhood that concerns you?"

3. Determine what you can do to help.

Is there anything you can do to help solve the problem? There may, in fact, be a simple answer that you don't want to overlook.

> ➤ If a student is having trouble in class with another student, move his seat.

> ➤ If a disruptive student is seated at the back of the class, consider moving her forward.

➤ Contact the parents if you feel a student needs additional help and support from home.

➤ Increase your positive support of the student, not just your corrective actions. Look at the first praiseworthy behavior after the conference, then send a positive note or behavior award home.

➤ A student may need academic help that you, a tutor, or a peer study buddy may be able to provide. Make that help available.

4. Determine how the student can improve his or her behavior.

Ask the student for his or her input concerning ways to improve the problem behavior. Share ideas. Keep in mind that students may not be willing or able to share their feelings about choosing a different behavior. If this is the case, help them by pointing out more appropriate behavior.

5. Agree on a course of action.

Combine your input with the student's input and agree upon a plan of action both of you can follow to improve the situation.

6. Clearly state that you expect the student to change his or her behavior.

At some point during the conference, you must let the student know that you expect the behavior to improve:

"I'm going to work with you to solve this problem, Leslie. You're a smart student, and I know you can behave responsibly. But you have to remember that fighting is not allowed at school. Any time you fight, you will be choosing to go to the principal."

7. Summarize the conference. Show your confidence!

Wrap up the conference by summarizing what was said. Most importantly, end with a note of confidence.

"I think we made a good start today, Romario. I know you can do better. Starting tomorrow, it will be different. I'm glad we had this talk."

✏️ It's Your Turn

Use the "Problem-Solving Conference Worksheet" on page 127 as a guide for conducting the conference and as a record of what was accomplished. If parents need to be involved at a future date, you will have documentation of steps already taken to solve the problem.

REPRODUCIBLE

Problem-Solving Conference Worksheet

Student's name _____ Date _____

1. Problem behavior the student is having (reason for conference): _____

2. Student input regarding problem (Why does the student think this problem is occurring?): _____

3. Steps the teacher can take to help solve the problem: _____

4. Actions the student can take to solve the problem: _____

5. Course of action agreed upon between teacher and student: _____

Follow-up and notes: _____

Assertive Discipline Elementary Workbook
© 2002 Solution Tree • www.solution-tree.com   127

Problem-Solving Conference Worksheet

Student's name _____ Date _____

1. Problem behavior the student is having (reason for conference): _____

_____

_____

_____

2. Student input regarding problem (Why does the student think this problem is occurring?): _____

_____

_____

3. Steps the teacher can take to help solve the problem: _____

_____

_____

_____

4. Actions the student can take to solve the problem: _____

_____

_____

_____

5. Course of action agreed upon between teacher and student: _____

_____

_____

_____

_____

_____

Follow-up and notes: _____

_____

_____

_____

_____

Develop an Individualized Behavior Plan

When your general classroom discipline plan is not effective with a student, you'll need to establish an individualized behavior plan for him or her. Such a plan is designed to adapt the concepts of your regular classroom discipline plan to meet the unique needs of a particular student.

An individualized behavior plan can help teach the student to behave responsibly and help you develop the positive relationship that so far may have been out of reach.

An individualized behavior plan includes:

➤ The specific behaviors expected of the student

➤ Meaningful corrective actions to be imposed if the student does not choose to engage in the appropriate behavior

➤ Meaningful supportive feedback to be given when the student does behave appropriately

Guidelines for Developing an Individualized Behavior Plan

1. Determine the behavior(s) you expect from the student.

Select one or two behaviors to work on at a time. Choose those that you believe are most important to the student's success. For example, if a student has a consistent problem with staying in his or her seat, the rule "Stay in your seat unless told to get up" would be an appropriate behavior to target.

2. Decide on meaningful corrective actions.

Often you will find that a difficult student reaches the same corrective action on the discipline hierarchy each day. For example, a student may reach the third step on the hierarchy every day and need to work away from the group on each of those days.

However, this student might always stop short of the corrective action that involves calling parents. The teacher can conclude that it may be effective to individualize this student's discipline plan so that the first time he or she disrupts instead of a reminder or isolation from the group, the student's parents are called immediately.

> **Note:** It may be appropriate with some difficult students to provide corrective actions that are not on your classroom discipline hierarchy. It may be necessary, for example, to keep a student in at recess or lunch even though the corrective action is not on your hierarchy.

Keep in mind that no matter what the corrective action is, it must always be meaningful to the student and, as always, provided consistently each time the student chooses to misbehave.

3. Determine more meaningful supportive feedback.

Your firmer, more meaningful corrective actions must always be balanced with increased supportive feedback. As always, begin with verbal recognition. Once you have implemented an individualized behavior plan, look for every opportunity to recognize the student's appropriate behavior. Make it a point to give positive attention to the student several times a day.

Back up your positive words with other forms of supportive feedback that you feel are appropriate, such as positive notes home or special privileges.

4. Keep parents informed.

A parent's involvement in an individualized behavior plan is critical. After all, it is likely that "Call parents" may be the first corrective action you use. Whenever you establish an individualized plan for a student, personal contact with the parent is vital. A phone call or face-to-face meeting is your best means of communicating the plan.

Here are the points you will want to cover in the meeting:

➤ Emphasize to the parents that your goal in establishing the individualized plan is to help the student learn more responsible behavior that will allow him or her to succeed in school.

➤ Explain the one or two behaviors that you are addressing. Let the parents know why you have chosen to emphasize these behaviors.

➤ Tell the parents what will happen the first time the student breaks one of these rules. Explain why you have chosen to use different corrective actions than those listed on the classroom discipline plan.

➤ Tell parents what will happen the second time a rule is broken.

➤ Ask if the parents have any questions regarding the use of the new corrective actions in the individualized plan.

➤ Explain the positive recognition you will give the student when he or she behaves appropriately. Reiterate the importance of reinforcing the student's efforts with consistent verbal recognition and other forms of support. Let the parents know that you are genuinely committed to the child's success.

➤ Tell the parents that you will provide a regular update to keep them informed of their child's progress. (In most cases, since parent contact will be part of the revised hierarchy, parents will hear if there's a problem. However, it's just as important to give a call or send a note when the student does behave appropriately.) Emphasize the importance of parents following through at home with positive reinforcement of their own. If appropriate, give parents a copy of the student's individualized behavior plan.

> *Note:* It is important that an individualized behavior plan be handled with sensitivity and caring. This is not a punitive effort; it is a plan tailor-made to meet a particular student's needs. Parents need to understand that this is a positive and proactive step, the goal of which is to help their child reach his or her potential. Let your words and attitude communicate this goal.

 **It's Your Turn**

Use the "Individualized Behavior Plan" form on page 131 to help prepare and record a student's individualized plan.

The individualized behavior plan should be presented to the student in a firm but empathetic manner. Difficult students need your assurance that you care, that you are there to help, and that disruptive behavior is not in their best interest.

 Refer to *Assertive Discipline, Third Edition,* for more information on developing an individualized behavior plan.

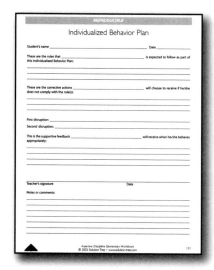

Individualized Behavior Plan

Student's name _____ Date _____

These are the rules that _____ is expected to follow as part of
this Individualized Behavior Plan:

_____

_____

_____

These are the corrective actions _____ will choose to receive if he/she
does not comply with the rule(s):

_____

_____

_____

First disruption: _____

Second disruption: _____

This is the supportive feedback _____ will receive when he/she behaves
appropriately:

_____

_____

_____

_____

_____
Teacher's signature   Date

Notes or comments:

_____

_____

_____

_____

_____

_____

Gain Support From Parents and Administrators

In Section 1, you learned the importance of sharing your classroom discipline plan with parents and with your administrator. These are important proactive measures that will help ensure that you get their support when you need it.

Responding to Problem Behaviors

Keep the following additional guidelines in mind as the year progresses and as behavior problems arise.

Take steps to respond on your own before asking for help.

Whenever appropriate, you should attempt to handle a student's disruptive behavior on your own before you speak to the parents or administrator about the situation. Both will want to know what actions you have taken to help the student. Assure them that you have already attempted to solve the problem on your own.

Remember, your goal is to teach the student to make good behavioral choices. If you involve parents or the administrator too soon, you are not allowing the student the opportunity to change his or her behavior.

Document a student's behavior and the steps you have taken to handle it.

When and if you do contact parents or an administrator, you will need accurate anecdotal documentation detailing when the problem has occurred and what steps you have taken. Documentation strengthens your position as a professional and communicates clearly to parents that these problems do exist.

Your anecdotal record should include the following information:

> Student's name and class

> Date, time, and place of incident

> Description of the problem

> Actions taken by the teacher

Keep these guidelines in mind when documenting problems:

Be specific. Keep away from vague opinions. Your statements should be based on factual, observable data.

Be consistent. Document problems each time they occur. Repeated occurrences may show a pattern and be helpful in solving the problem.

Name: Jonathan Stein **Class:** Room 4

Date: 4/24/02

Problem: During math, Jonathan twice pushed Kerry's book on the floor.

Actions taken: Moved Jonathan to the front of the classroom for the duration of the afternoon.

It's Your Turn

Use the reproducible Behavior Documentation Cards on page 134 to record anecdotal data about a student's behavior. Consider duplicating the cards on index stock for added durability. Fold them in half with the student's name facing forward. Alternatively, use documentation spreadsheets on your computer and include the suggested information.

Behavior Documentation Cards

Student _____ Home Phone _____

Parent's Name _____ Work _____

Parent's Name _____ Work _____

Date _____ Time _____ Place _____

Description of Problem/Incident: _____

_____

Action Taken: _____

Date _____ Time _____ Place _____

Description of Problem/Incident: _____

_____

Action Taken: _____

Date _____ Time _____ Place _____

Description of Problem/Incident: _____

_____

Action Taken: _____

FOLD HERE

Student _____ Home Phone _____

Parent's Name _____ Work _____

Parent's Name _____ Work _____

Date _____ Time _____ Place _____

Description of Problem/Incident: _____

_____

Action Taken: _____

Date _____ Time _____ Place _____

Description of Problem/Incident: _____

_____

Action Taken: _____

Date _____ Time _____ Place _____

Description of Problem/Incident: _____

_____

Action Taken: _____

FOLD HERE

Assertive Discipline Elementary Workbook
© 2002 Solution Tree Press • solution-tree.com

Getting Support From Parents When a Problem Arises

How do you know when you should contact a parent about a problem? Some situations are very clear: severe fighting, extreme emotional distress, or a student who refuses to work or turn in homework. Don't think twice about involving parents when these situations occur.

What about the day-to-day instances that may not be so obvious? If you are uncertain about contacting a parent, use the "Your Own Child" test. This test will put you in the position of the parent, and help clarify whether or not parental help is called for.

Take the "Your Own Child" test.

1. Assume you have a child of your own the same age as the student in question.

2. If your child was having the same problem in school as that student, would you want to be called?

3. If the answer is yes, call the parent. If the answer is no, do not call the parent.

Before you pick up a phone or meet with parents, outline what you are going to say. These notes will help you think through and clarify the points you want to make. Having the notes in front of you while you're speaking will help you communicate more effectively.

It's Your Turn

Assertive Discipline in Action! Cue Card #12 (see page 136) lists all the points you'll want to cover when contacting a parent about a problem. Reproduce and laminate this cue card and keep it available for use. Use the reproducible "Parent Contact Worksheet" on page 137 to help you prepare for your meeting and to record pertinent data after the meeting.

Cue Card #12

Contacting Parents About a Problem

Follow these steps when contacting a parent about a problem.

Step 1: Begin with a statement of concern.

Let the parent know that you care about the student.

Step 2: Describe the specific problem and present pertinent documentation.

Explain in specific, observable terms what the student did.

Step 3: Describe what you have done.

Explain exactly how you have dealt with the problem so far. Make sure that the parent is aware of the steps you have already taken to solve the problem.

Step 4: Get parental input on the problem.

Listen carefully to what the parent has to say. Here are some questions you may want to ask:

"Has your child had similar problems in the past?"

"Why do you feel your child is having these problems at school?"

"Is there something (divorce, separation, siblings, a move) going on at home that could be affecting your child's behavior?"

Step 5: Get parental input on how to solve the problem.

Parents may have a good idea that could help solve a specific problem. Ask for input, and listen carefully to the responses.

Step 6: Tell the parent what you will do to help solve the problem.

You've already explained what you have previously done. Let the parent know exactly what specific actions you are going to take now.

Step 7: Explain what you need the parent to do to solve the problem.

Clearly and carefully explain specifically what you would like the parent to do.

Step 8: Let the parent know you are confident that the problem can be worked out.

Wrap up the conversation or meeting on a positive note.

Step 9: Tell the parent that there will be follow-up contact from you.

The parent needs to know that you are going to stay involved. Provide this reassurance by giving a specific date for a follow-up call or note.

Step 10: Recap the conference.

Clarify all agreements. Restate or write down what you are going to do and what the parent is going to do. Keep this information in your files.

© 2002 Solution Tree

Assertive Discipline Elementary Workbook
© 2002 Solution Tree Press • solution-tree.com

Parent Contact Worksheet

Student's name _____ Date of call or meeting _____

Parent or guardian _____

Home phone _____ Work phone _____

In the spaces below, write the important points you will cover with the parent, as well as points made during the meeting or conversation.

1. Begin with a statement of concern. _____

_____

2. Describe the specific problem (state in observable terms). _____

_____

3. Review what you have already done to try to solve the problem. _____

_____

4. Get parental input on how to solve the problem. Record parent comments. _____

_____

5. Present your solutions to the problem.

What you will do: _____

_____

What you want the parent to do: _____

_____

6. Express confidence once again in your ability to solve the problem.

7. Arrange for follow-up contact.

Notes: _____

_____

_____

_____

_____

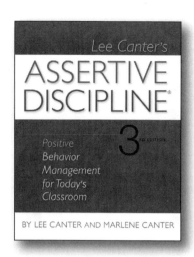

Assertive Discipline®: Positive Behavior Management for Today's Classroom
Lee Canter and Marlene Canter

Third Edition! Employ a proven three-step approach for positive behavior management by creating a classroom discipline plan that includes: rules all students must follow; supportive feedback for students who follow the rules; and corrective actions for student who don't follow the rules. **BKF182**

Teacher's Plan Book Plus #1: Assertive Discipline®
Lee Canter

Strengthen your discipline efforts with behavior management tips and reminders used by more than 500,000 teachers. Each week you'll find an Assertive Discipline implementation tip, a motivating positive reinforcement idea, space for jotting daily reminders, and room to record specific discipline notes. **BKF194**

Teacher's Plan Book Plus #2: Assertive Discipline®
Lee Canter

Integrate advanced behavior management ideas into your curriculum using strategies from the proven Assertive Discipline program. By mapping out the steps you will take each week to ensure a well-managed classroom, you will increase your effectiveness and the success of your students. **BKF195**

Classroom Management for Academic Success
Lee Canter

This groundbreaking resource details effective management strategies you can implement from day one so that all students achieve in the classroom. Teacher-tested, research-based strategies create a classroom in which children learn free from the distraction of disruptive behavior. **BKF209**

The Four Keys to Effective Classroom and Behavior Management: Building Community, Motivation, Responsibility, and School Safety
Richard L. Curwin and Allen N. Mendler

Explore four skill areas essential to establishing a safe, supportive learning environment. In this video series, Curwin and Mendler demonstrate proven, research-based strategies in dramatized scenes and actual classroom settings. Deliver the material over a 2-day in-service period or in extended intervals. **VIF093**

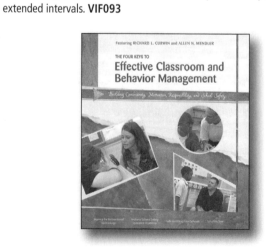